Basics *for* Believers

Foundational Truths
to Guide Your Life

William L. Thrasher, Jr.

MOODY PRESS
CHICAGO

To Mary,
my wonderful wife and
beloved companion,
my co-laborer in serving Christ
and His kingdom, and
my fellow sojourner
on the way to heaven

Contents

Section 3
GOD WITH US

Section 4
A GODLY LIFE

Section 5
AN ORGANIZED LIFE

Section 6
A FOCUSED LIFE

Foreword

As our lives become marked by increasing complexity, there is something very refreshing about simplicity. For every dozen books that leave us asking, "*What did that mean?*" we might find one that is clear, concise, immediately understandable, and obviously applicable. This book passes these tests of readability, and Bill Thrasher writes from his personal experience—years of working out his salvation in the ebb and flow of life.

Not only are we given practical biblical insight, but we are encouraged to believe that, with God's help, we can make fresh discoveries and vital progress in each of these areas.

As with most areas of life, successful Christian living is the product of learning by God's enabling to *do the basics well most of the time.* If the reader fails to make progress, it will not be due to an absence of helpful information, but on account of a lack of application. This book is a rich compendium of practical insight, helping us to be doers of the Word and not hearers only. You should keep a volume on your desk or in the glove compartment of your car. As you stand in your teenagers' bedrooms, resolve to buy them one for their birthday, or sooner if need be!

Alistair Begg
Senior Pastor
Parkside Church
Chagrin Falls, Ohio

Acknowledgments

With each day added to the eighteen years since I came to a saving faith in the Lord Jesus Christ, I become more and more acutely aware of the special place the Holy Spirit of God assumes in my daily life. That reality has increasingly dominated my thoughts over this past year as I've developed and written this book. Only through the guidance, prompting, and teaching of the Holy Spirit has this book been made possible. I stand in amazement that the triune God continues to use an insignificant "clay pot" such as me to share His precious truths. To God be all the glory!

I also want to acknowledge those wonderful pastors, teachers, and authors God has used to help me along in my spiritual journey. Only God knows the glorious rewards that await each one of these saints in heaven for their faithful service to our Lord. I thank God for the role they have played in the furtherance of the work of His kingdom.

My deepest gratitude goes to Greg Thornton and Dennis Shere for their encouragement and suggestions in this book project, but even more for the examples of godliness and holiness they live out daily in the exercise of their leadership.

I would also like to thank Tracy Sumner for his valuable input on final editing and to Cheryl Dunlop for the work of bringing all the pieces together.

Last, I want to acknowledge my partner in this project, my wife, Mary, whose editing made the finished product more readable. Her help on verse selection and her being my in-house critic—as well as my greatest encouragement—were truly blessings. She has demonstrated a true servant's heart in that the one with more talent served the one with less. Thank you.

Introduction

As John Bunyan explained in his famous allegory *Pilgrim's Progress*, the life of a believer is a journey. It begins at the moment of the new birth and advances with its ups and downs until we finally leave this earth. This journey is meant to be preparation for eternity and has profound implications for both this life and the life to come.

Unfortunately, because of the culture and the environment in which we live today, numerous believers are not grounded in Scripture, nor are they familiar with many of the major subjects of the Christian faith. Others, due to the frantic pace of today's society, have neglected any real development of a strong spiritual life. The journey for new believers is just beginning. What they need is a very simple map that will point them in the right direction and guide them to the best resources for the long trek ahead.

Theology, once referred to as the "queen of the sciences," has, for the most part, come to be seen as a subject to be avoided. In many cases, habits developed today are insignificant rather than important, producing a shallow and sad example of life rather than what our Creator God intended for us.

My goal in writing this book is to present a simple, foundational review of many of the basic truths of the Christian faith, written in such a way as to keep them short, understandable, and to the point. Included are a number of topics that play significant roles in the way we live our lives. As the reader progresses through these pages, I hope that he or she will rediscover the awesome story of God revealed in the Bible. I also hope the reader will find some tools that provide motivation and direction for an exciting, vibrant life in Christ.

In order to provide the biblical foundation to the topic, I have given a Scripture verse at the beginning of each theme. I have incorporated at the end of every topic an application tool called "Action Step," which is written to encourage readers to put what they have learned into practice and to measure their progress as they grow. Also included is the title of a book related to each of the fifty-two topics discussed, furnishing the reader with an expanded coverage of the subject. This should be an excellent way for the reader to build on to these simple presentations.

The design of this book is intended to afford the reader many different ways in which to use it. One approach that some may find helpful has been spelled out in the appendix titled "How to Use This Book." Some will read it in the typical fashion: from beginning to end over a few days. Others, after reviewing the eight sections, may want to concentrate their reading in one specific section first, then skip around according to their needs and interests. Another approach for those who don't read a lot is to read one topic per day. Since each topic can be read in a short time, this may be an ideal approach for many. For those who read very little, one topic per week will work fine. I also encourage you to read the appendix entitled "Tools for the Journey," which will enable many readers to discover a system that will greatly assist them in applying the various actions recommended in each section.

My hope and prayer is that you find these short "basics for believers" to be like a glass of cool, refreshing water for a distracted, weary, and thirsty soul. I hope they will cause you to thirst for more and more. Just as important, I pray you will use the Scripture verses and the action steps, as well as the recommended books, to further your own journey as you grow spiritually.

Learning to live the abundant life in Christ is truly a magnificent experience. I wholeheartedly recommend it and ask you to seriously consider taking this step yourself.

Section 1

GOD OF ALL

1
God

· ✂ ·

In the beginning God created the heaven and the earth (Genesis 1:1).

Within the past ten years startling discoveries have been made concerning the universe of which our planet earth is a part. With each new discovery it becomes obvious that the cosmos (another term for universe) is much greater in size than scientists have previously thought. Even more mind-boggling is the fact that the cosmos is still expanding! New galaxies are being formed, and billions of new stars are taking shape within those new galaxies.

The more we discover and learn about the cosmos, the more awesome it becomes, and, in some ways, the more insignificant we feel. Yet the answer to the mystery of the universe is no farther away than the Bible. Here is what the Bible says is the answer: Everything began with God.

If we are to ultimately understand life and its purpose, the world in which we live, and why we exist, it must start with God. The Creator God existed before there was anything. At some point in time God created more than 100 billion galaxies. Think about that for a moment—100 billion galaxies! He has created everything within those galaxies, including the earth. Within the earth's galaxy, the Milky Way, there are more than 200 billion stars.

· · · · ·

God created all living things. Most significantly, God created human beings in His image. God desired fellowship with His creatures, but, unfortunately, an event occurred that broke this fellowship. God did not leave this condition unresolved, however, and the account of what God did and how this story has been played out in history are contained in the instruction book on how to know God. It is called the Bible. God has wonderfully and mercifully provided this truth so that we can learn about Him and know Him and fulfill what has always been His purpose for our lives.

Once we comprehend in some small way the infinite, almighty God, we can begin to see ourselves for what we really are—fallen creatures alienated from a holy God by sin. Only then can we begin to discover what we can become by God's grace.

ACTION STEP:

Set aside some time and ask God to help you begin the process of learning more about Him. Pray that He will direct you in this area and bless your efforts. Search the book of Genesis and list the mighty works and wonders God performed for His people.

FOR FURTHER READING:

Knowing God
chapter 1, pp. 17–23
J. I. Packer

2
The Trinity

· ❧ ·

Then God said, "Let Us make man in Our image, according to Our likeness" (Genesis 1:26 NKJV).

As we begin an attempt to come to grips with the Creator God, it is wonderful to learn that this magnificent and merciful God has revealed to mankind that He exists in three distinct persons. The Creator God is one in essence (that is, His ultimate nature) but at the same time is three different persons. It is exciting to realize that before time was, God existed in perfect fellowship and blessed communion within the Godhead.

The doctrine of the Trinity is brought to light as one studies the Bible, and it is very clear that the Creator God exists in unity as three persons—the Father, the Son, and the Holy Spirit—in one Godhead. All three are equal in power, majesty, glory, and sovereignty. Each has accepted an ordered role of organization, but each is equal with all divine attributes. Since the Trinity is so beyond our understanding, it is another unmistakable demonstration that this revelation was not from man. Beyond this biblical disclosure, no one can further explain or comprehend this wondrous truth other than to see how the various roles of the Godhead come to impact us humans. Many "types" or "likes" have been employed attempting to provide a more explicit insight of the Trinity, but all have failed. The Trinity is unlike anything within our intellectual

· · · · ·

grasp, beyond everything and everyone. We must finally accept that God is as He is—one God in three persons.

Each person of the Godhead has been revealed to some extent in the Bible. A closer examination of each will help us to better understand their functions. God the Father was involved with creation and is ruler of all things. He is the author of our election and the designer of the plan of redemption. God the Son submitted to the incarnation by becoming a man so He could secure our redemption by bearing our sins at the Crucifixion. God the Holy Spirit convicts us of sin, calls us to redemption, and guides, leads, and teaches us in the way of holy living. The more we learn of these distinctive roles, the more overwhelming God becomes to us.

ACTION STEP:

As you take time to think about the subject of the Trinity, ask God to help you to accept the mystery and the incomprehensible truth of its reality. Rejoice in the revelation we have of God. Make a list of the verses in Scriptures related to the Trinity.

FOR FURTHER READING:

Foundations of the Christian Faith: A Comprehensive & Readable Theology
chapter 10, pp. 109–16
James Montgomery Boice

3
Names & Attributes of God

· ✀ ·

And God said to Moses, "I AM WHO I AM." And He said, "Thus you shall say to the children of Israel, I AM has sent me to you" (Exodus 3:14 NKJV).

As we approach the subject of God, it is helpful to make some general statements that provide some points of reference. God, in one sense, is unknowable and incomprehensible because He is God. Yet in the Bible He has made Himself known through special revelation regarding His nature, His attributes, and His names. All the attributes of God apply equally to the Father, the Son, and the Holy Spirit. God has revealed Himself through the person of His Son, the Lord Jesus Christ. As we learn of Christ, we learn of God. As we look at some of the names and characteristics of God, we can better understand who He reveals Himself to be.

Jehovah is the name that states God is eternal. He has no beginning and no end. He is not subject to time. Jehovah God is self-existent. He has no origin; He was not created. He is independent of everything but Himself. God is self-sufficient. He has no need of anything; He is sufficient unto Himself. Jehovah God is immutable. He is unchangeable and unchanging. He is complete.

Elohim is the name of God that presents Him as the almighty God who is sovereign over all things. He created everything out of nothing. Elohim is also the God of the covenant. He has provided the means for restoration of the fallen race. The name Elohim is plural in the original, which allows for the involvement of the three persons of the Godhead in the drama of the events preparing for redemption.

The Bible reveals that God is infinite. He has no bounds or limits. He is everywhere, not limited by space or time. God is holy. He is pure and perfect. He is the standard of holiness. God is love. He seeks good for those He loves. God's love is pure, perfect, and true.

All of God's attributes are in perfect balance because they are each complete in Him. As we reflect on these truths, our finite minds are overwhelmed. God is truly awesome.

ACTION STEP:

Make a list of attributes ascribed to God in the Bible. These can be found in any complete book on theology. Use your list when you pray and thank God for His wonderful attributes.

FOR FURTHER READING:

Names of God
chapters 1 and 2, pp. 7–29
Nathan Stone

4

The Lord Jesus Christ

He is the image of the invisible God, the firstborn over all creation. For by Him all things were created that are in heaven and that are on earth, visible and invisible, whether thrones or dominions or principalities or powers. All things were created through Him and for Him (Colossians 1:15–16 NKJV).

My family and I have enjoyed some very special opportunities to travel to and live in other parts of the world. Those journeys have left us with many treasured memories and experiences. They were times that offered exposure to new cultures, tasks, and people. Overall, these were delightful seasons of our lives that granted us many unique adventures. But at the end of each business assignment, the time came for us to be going home. Every journey comes to an end.

It's that way with our time on earth too. One day, this life will be over for each of us and we will enter eternity. At that moment, the way we related to the person of Jesus Christ in this life will determine our eternal destiny. For the believer, Christ will become the sum of everything to be praised, honored, and worshiped. We will prostrate ourselves before Him and give Him tribute for everything that is the result of the new creation He has made us to be. We will acknowledge that all praiseworthy things we have done are by His power and grace. For the first time, we will see Him without the veil of sin. We will see the wounds inflicted on Him for our salvation. There will be no question of identity—we will know Christ and Christ will know us. We will see our Redeemer, our Lord, and our God. We will be reunited with our loved ones who have died in Christ and meet those wonderful saints we have come to know and love through our Bible study. Oh, what a happy day!

The book of Revelation, the final book of the Bible, gives readers two portraits of the wondrous Lamb of God. When we no longer look through dimly colored glass, then we shall behold Him as He truly is—the light of the world in whom all things exist, in whom and for whom all things were created, by whom all things are sustained, and who alone is to be worshiped. We will behold God with us forever.

The other picture of Christ in Revelation is the judge of all, the One who will execute final judgment on all the unredeemed, the devil and his angels, and on sin itself. All the universe will be purged of anything sinful, ushering in the new paradise. We will begin an eternal, never-ending time to learn and worship and fellowship with God. Heaven will be beyond anything we can imagine.

ACTION STEP:

Make a point to read the book of Revelation. Outline the key points covered in chapters 4 and 5. Ask yourself where you are in your walk with the Lord. Purpose in your heart to do the things that will help you grow in Christ, then do the things that will make that happen.

FOR FURTHER READING:

The Glory of Christ
chapter 33, pp. 459–75
Peter Lewis

5

The Holy Spirit

So I advise you to live according to your new life in the Holy Spirit. Then you won't be doing what your sinful nature craves (Galatians 5:16).

From my earliest recollections, I remember being exposed to the Christian faith and its message of hope and deliverance in the gospel. There was never any doubt in my mind about Jesus Christ, His work on the cross, or the reality of heaven and hell. As a young boy of six or seven I heard the gospel preached and asked Jesus to come into my heart. I thought I had been born again, but I now know there was an absence of the convicting work of the Holy Spirit, the third person of the Trinity. I clearly wanted to avoid hell, but I did not really comprehend my need to repent as a lost sinner. I had a form of religion, but I did not have a saving faith that transforms lives. I exhibited many outward signs of a believer, but in reality the presence of the Holy Spirit living within my heart was missing.

In October 1980, by the power of the Holy Spirit, I was raised from spiritual death and made alive to God. I became a new creation and my life was changed. Everything about me was affected—my thoughts, habits, speech, and desires. I was made aware of my own sinfulness and of the sin all around me. I began to see the world from a biblical perspective. The Bible was suddenly alive and clear to me. My eyes were opened and my heart, mind, and will became sensitive to God's direction.

This transformation was the result of the work of the precious Holy Spirit of God. He became my teacher through the Word of God, encouraging me to study and learn and pray. He took the role of my guide, pointing me toward Christ and His kingdom. He encouraged and helped me, and, most of all, He comforted me. He worked through my mind, feelings, and will.

It is the Holy Spirit's work to carry out the process of sanctification (becoming more godly and less worldly) in the lives of believers. His goal is to conform us to the image of Christ, to make us holy even as He is holy. His role is to abide in us and convict us of sin, moving us to continued repentance.

Now I understand so clearly the truth from the Word of God. Just as it is not possible to have sanctification without regeneration (the new birth), it is not possible to have regeneration without sanctification. As believers, we can slow and delay our consecration (being set aside for God's purposes), but the Holy Spirit will bring it to pass if we are true children of God. When that happens, there will be more evidences of the fruit of the Spirit and there will be less and less of the flesh present in our daily lives. Some will grow strong and be used mightily by the Lord; others will have slow but steady growth and over time will achieve a positive impact for Christ. Unfortunately, there will be some who will remain childish with only modest growth and will miss a big part of their calling.

As believers, we all have the responsibility to work hard to prove that we really are among those God has called and chosen in the power of the Holy Spirit.

ACTION STEP:

Read and study the fifth chapter of Galatians. Pay special attention to verses 16–24, which deal with life in the Holy Spirit. Look for areas of your life in which you are not allowing the Holy Spirit to work. Pray to submit them to God.

FOR FURTHER READING:

The Mystery of the Holy Spirit
chapter 2, pp. 22–32
R. C. Sproul

6

The Bible

The grass withers, the flower fades, but the word of our God stands forever (Isaiah 40:8 NASB).

The Bible is the very Word of God, supernatural in its origin, inspired by God, and without error. All issues and discussions concerning doctrine should start with the Bible. The Bible is God's instruction book on life and on how to have a personal and everlasting relationship with the Creator God. There is no way finite creatures can know anything of an infinite God unless He chooses to reveal Himself. The Bible discloses God to man and explains man to himself.

Some might ask: How can I be certain that the Bible is God's revelation to mankind? Let's briefly examine this question.

The Bible has endured for thousands of years, yet it is as fresh and applicable today as it was when it was first written. It is timeless because it is the Word of God. It is also limitless in its applications to life, and its source of truth cannot be exhausted. As more and more archeological discoveries are made, more and more the accuracy of the Bible is reinforced. Many facts that were once brought into question have now been proven correct by new discoveries. The way the Bible reveals God could only come from God, and the way man is understood and presented could only come from the One who knows all things. The prophecies of the Bible clearly demonstrate the omniscience of its author. And, finally, the complete unity of the Bible declares its author to be divine.

The impact and influence of the Bible on individuals continue to demonstrate its supernatural power. It convicts people of sin and shows the way of pardon from sin. It is the story of God's love for fallen humanity. Its truth leads the way to salvation. It directs us in the path of sanctification, and its revelation of heaven and hell is the reality of our final destination.

Arthur Pink's summary in his book, *The Divine Inspiration of the Bible,* says it well: "The Bible is the Book to live by and the Book to die by. Therefore read it to be wise, believe it to be safe, practice it to be holy." If we are to know God in a deeper way and understand His will for our lives, we must be diligent in becoming people of His Word.

ACTION STEP:

Set a goal to read one chapter a day from the book of Proverbs for one month. Keep a simple record to measure your success using a calendar or making an easy chart from one to thirty-one and marking your progress each day with a check mark as you read. At the end of the month, review and repeat the procedure for another month.

FOR FURTHER READING:

The Divine Inspiration of the Bible
chapters 1 and 2, pp. 11–19
Arthur W. Pink

7

Doctrine

All Scripture is given by inspiration of God, and is profitable for doctrine, for reproof, for correction, for instruction in righteousness (2 Timothy 3:16 NKJV).

Having grown up in a family associated with the construction industry, I learned early in life of the value and use of blueprints. Blueprints are the detailed instructions on how to build something. They can be very simple or extraordinarily complex. They provide a visual layout of how things are connected, the specific materials involved, and the sequence involved in the work. Blueprints are indispensable to good construction. In the Christian life, the same can be said of doctrine.

Doctrine is a branch of knowledge or a system of beliefs. For the believer in Christ, this system is based on and drawn from God's special revelation unfolded in the Bible. Doctrines address specific subjects within the Christian faith. Some of the doctrines of the Christian faith are: God, man, sin, Jesus Christ, salvation, and the Holy Spirit. Focusing on a specific doctrine helps us to better understand the subject as well as the practical implications of that subject as it relates to our lives.

Some of our Christian doctrines are limited because God has not revealed all the details about them in Scripture. A good example of this is the doctrine of creation. God made it clear that He created all things, but very little is detailed in the Bible as to how and why. Yet, all that we need to know has been disclosed to us.

In contrast, the doctrine of redemption (God reuniting us with Himself) runs throughout most of the Bible and is clearly a major doctrine of Scripture. The doctrine of redemption provides a classic example of why the study and organization of our beliefs is so beneficial. Without a focus on key doctrines, much of the truth of the Bible might be lost. An excellent analogy is to look at the Bible as God's library for man, to be used to research and assimilate understanding about key subjects of life. One of the most exciting things you will discover is the inexhaustibility of the Word of God. You will be amazed as you begin the process of searching this wonderful Book to better understand the key doctrines of our faith.

ACTION STEP:

Make a list of subjects you have often thought about that relate to your faith, such as: man, God, sin, the devil, angels, worship, and heaven. Locate a Bible with a concordance, an alphabetical index of the principle words used in Scripture. Look up each of the topics and record the verses that are referenced. The study of these verses will lead to other references, all of which will help you to begin to understand the truth of a specific doctrine.

FOR FURTHER READING:

Essential Truths of the Christian Faith: 100 Doctrines in Plain Language
preface and introduction
R. C. Sproul

Section 2

GOD FOR ALL

8

The Fall

As it is written: There is none righteous, no, not one; there is none who understands; there is none who seeks after God (Romans 3:10–11 NKJV).

When one reads a daily newspaper or one of the weekly news magazines or watches the evening news, the realization of the horrible presence of evil in this world is inescapable. The degrees to which evil affects different people may vary, but evil is no respecter of persons, groups, races, or genders. Psychologists have suggested various explanations for the problem, but their reasoning never seems to fully clarify this universal condition. Others attribute the problem of evil to the result of one's environment.

The Bible, in contrast, has told us where evil came from and detailed how it was introduced to mankind. Evil is the result of the introduction of sin into the human race. This event is called the Fall.

When God created Adam, He made him to be representative of all of mankind. God placed Adam in the Garden of Eden along with his wife, Eve. God laid down the instructions of life for Adam, and they included a warning against disobedience to these rules. Adam, however, disobeyed these instructions and fell from his proper relationship with God. When Adam chose to disobey God, sin entered into Adam and into all of Adam's race. This was the consequence of the Fall. Fellowship with God was destroyed and a curse was placed on Adam and Eve, the earth itself, and Satan. Death entered the world. From the present until the end of time, Satan will be allowed a limited amount of influence, sin will flourish, and all of creation will need to be reclaimed from final destruction.

Wonderfully, God was not surprised by the Fall. He had designed a plan to bring about three miraculous events that would provide the way of victory over sin. What miracles are those? That Christ came, that He died, and that He rose from the grave.

ACTION STEP:

Read Romans 5:12–20 and relate how these verses bring expanded understanding to Genesis 3.

FOR FURTHER READING:

The Serpent of Paradise: The Incredible Story of How Satan's Rebellion Serves God's Purposes
chapter 1, pp. 13–22
Erwin W. Lutzer

9

Sin

*For all have sinned and fall short of the glory of God
(Romans 3:23 NKJV).*

One of the most frightening words in the English language is the word *cancer.* The reason for this fear is that almost everyone has had a friend or family member struck down by this devastating disease. Cancer can have tragic results.

In contrast, the word *sin* usually does not evoke much reaction or concern, yet the Bible speaks extensively on the subject. Sin is the root of all the terrible things that have occurred in the history of mankind. Sin is the reason for death and disease. Sin created a need for a hell. As one contemplates the subject of sin, it becomes obvious that this is a critical issue that everyone should strive to understand.

What is sin? Sin is anything that is contrary to the holy character of God. It is anything that corrupts holiness. This definition indicates two things clearly: Anything done that is not consistent with God's holiness is sin, and anything not done that God requires of us is sin.

An understanding of God's standard makes it apparent that everyone has fallen so far below His requirement that degrees of sin are not the issue. A term for sin used in the New Testament is "to miss the mark." If the mark is the moon, even the best of people have only reached the treetops.

Since the fall of mankind in the Garden of Eden, everyone is born a sinner. We sin because we are sinners. Sin brings with it God's condemnation. Everyone who sins is under God's sentence of eternal damnation. The Bible also indicates that as sinners we are slaves to sin. We will never be completely free from sinning in this life.

Sin is a serious condition with eternal consequences. It is clear that in ourselves we have no real solution. Our condition is hopeless. Apart from a miracle, the human race would be doomed. Fortunately, there was a miracle. It is called the Incarnation. That means that God took on the form of a man and lived among us.

ACTION STEP:

Make a list of things you might have come to tolerate that are clearly defined in Scripture as sin. For example, gossip, lying, laziness, or envy. Continue your list for one month, then take the next month to pray about and endeavor to eliminate these sinful habits from your own life.

FOR FURTHER READING:

The Vanishing Conscience
chapter 10, pp. 197–209
John F. MacArthur, Jr.

10

The Incarnation

······························∘⌀∘·····························

And the Word became flesh and dwelt among us, and we beheld His glory, the glory as of the only begotten of the Father, full of grace and truth (John 1:14 NKJV).

One of the three miracles that God performed to solve the sin problem is called the Incarnation. This event occurred when God began the process that would break the consequences of the Fall and of sin. God, through the power of the Holy Spirit, by way of a virgin, became a man—and yet remained God.

Jesus Christ, the Son, the second person of the Trinity, became the God-man—fully God and fully man. The Bible tells us He was sent by the Father, conceived by the Holy Spirit, and born of the Virgin Mary. God became an infant. He lived and grew, just as other children born of man, but without sin, because He was holy. The Bible tells us that even as a young child, He was unique. He was "about my Father's business" (Luke 2:49).

As Jesus matured, He was tempted but didn't yield to those temptations. He felt all the same emotions humans do so that He could fully relate to us. He endured the great trial of testing by Satan himself, yet He successfully resisted. Jesus Christ ultimately endured the gross injustice of the religious leaders of His day, who displayed the vileness of hypocrisy and hate, and who influenced Pilate to sentence Him to death. Still, His life was sinless.

· · · · ·

Jesus Christ lived a perfect life, obedient to all His heavenly Father called Him to do, so that He could be the spotless Lamb of God, the sacrifice for sin. He was the Second Adam. The first Adam sinned and brought a curse; the Second Adam, Christ, lived a blameless life and brought blessing and salvation. Jesus, the Son of God, came to represent God's elect and to reclaim them from their lost condition, to provide for them that which was impossible for them to furnish for themselves. Christ's becoming man and living a sinless life was the first of three steps that were necessary in order for sin and death to be defeated.

ACTION STEP:

Set a goal over the next week to read and think about the incarnation of Jesus Christ recorded in the books of Matthew, Mark, and Luke. Also, focus on what Jesus went through as a man.

FOR FURTHER READING:

The Glory of Christ: Encounter the Majesty of the Lord of Lords
chapters 1 and 2, pp. 12–40
R. C. Sproul

11

The Crucifixion

For God so loved the world that He gave His only begotten Son, that whoever believes in Him should not perish but have everlasting life (John 3:16 NKJV).

The second great miracle in the process of salvation for sinners was the event called the Crucifixion. That is the event Christians celebrate every year on Good Friday. The Bible reveals from the beginning the need for the shedding of blood in order to atone for or make right for the sins of those forgiven. Sin required a sacrifice. The story of the Passover in the Bible from the book of Exodus is a wonderful example that God used to portray to us the coming Lamb of God who would take away the sins of the world. The stories of the tabernacle and the temple also point to the ultimate and final sacrifice in Jesus Christ.

A sinless sacrifice was the only way for God to balance His holiness and His love toward sinful mankind. God in Christ became that spotless sacrifice and demonstrated His holiness and love. Jesus Christ endured the wrath of God for the sins of His people and laid down His life because of His great love for us.

The Crucifixion also exposes the evil and wickedness in the hearts of men. Jesus Christ was the only completely innocent person who ever lived, yet the religious people of that day, together with those in authority, beat Him, cursed Him, and nailed Him to the cross.

Not only does the Crucifixion proclaim the grace, love, and mercy of God, it also discloses the wisdom and power of God. God's wisdom is manifested in the Cross, for this plan of redemption was formed before the foundation of the world. God knew man would be powerless to save himself after the Fall, and He understood what would be needed to restore man to fellowship with Him. God's power was exhibited in the fact that His Son's death secured salvation for all who believe, and it humbles all who come to faith in Him by way of the Cross. The Crucifixion defeated the devil and all the powers at his disposal. The dominion of sin in the life of the redeemed was broken and the ability to live a victorious life in Christ was restored.

Only God could resolve the problem of sin. Salvation is all of God. The wonder of the Son of God dying to reconcile sinful people to Himself is remarkable. The more we come to comprehend the magnitude of what was accomplished by Jesus Christ on the cross at Calvary, the more sacred and solemn this remembrance becomes. Each year as we grow in our understanding of what it cost God in Christ for our redemption, the more Good Friday will become one of the most significant days of the year.

ACTION STEP:

Read the story of the Crucifixion in the four Gospels. Write down a comparison of what is revealed in each one. Become familiar with the events that surround this miraculous event.

FOR FURTHER READING:

The Cross of Christ
chapter 7, pp. 167–75
John R. W. Stott

12

The Resurrection

*Jesus said to her, "I am the resurrection and the life. He who believes in Me, though he may die, he shall live"
(John 11:25 NKJV).*

The thing that humanity longs for above all other things is forgiveness. Everybody needs forgiveness. The history of man is filled with examples of attempts to do things to bring forgiveness from God. This is the result of the conscience God has given us. Many spend their lives trying to earn it through all types of religious activities or self works. Others spend their time trying to bury the feeling of needing forgiveness through various distractions or preoccupations. Some finally condemn themselves to despair and live out a sad, tormented, hopeless existence. Sadly, they have missed the only hope mankind has ever had for forgiveness, peace, and joy. It lies in the truth of the Resurrection, the third great miracle of God in the process of salvation.

God demonstrated through the Resurrection that He was completely satisfied with the sacrifice of His only begotten Son, Jesus Christ, for sin. Therefore, when we believe in Christ, we have full, complete, and eternal forgiveness. We have assurance. We have peace with God because we are forgiven.

God exhibited the absolute certainty through the Resurrection that Jesus Christ was His Son, that what had been foreshadowed in the Old Testament prophecies were fulfilled in Christ, and that what Jesus had said would

occur did happen. Jesus told everyone that after three days God would raise Him up from the dead, and He did! In the Resurrection, believers have assurance that they can live victorious lives in Christ. Jesus won the victory over sin and death. Through the presence of the Holy Spirit, we can live our lives in a way that is pleasing to God. The Resurrection assures believers that they have eternal life.

The Resurrection began a new creation, and with the addition of every new believer, one more part of this new creation is added. Someday this present world and the present heavens will be destroyed and replaced with a new heaven and new earth. The completion of the new creation will be accomplished.

This world yearns for peace, love, joy, and forgiveness. It is found in only one place: in the birth, the death, and the resurrection of Jesus Christ. This is the way, this is the truth, and this is the life.

ACTION STEP:

Read the account of the Resurrection in the four Gospels. Make a comparison of the key facts and events in writing. Also read the fifteenth chapter of 1 Corinthians to see how Paul expounds on the key doctrines of the Resurrection.

FOR FURTHER READING:

He Still Moves Stones
chapter 19, pp. 182–88
Max Lucado

13
The Gospel

· · · · · · · · · · · · · · · · · · ❧ · · · · · · · · · · · · · · · · · · ·

For I am not ashamed of the gospel of Christ, for it is the power of God to salvation for everyone who believes, for the Jew first and also for the Greek (Romans 1:16 NKJV).

It has been recorded that General George S. Patton, the World War II hero who conquered a large part of Europe, demanded that the soldiers who served under him be able at any time to clearly and correctly state the objective of the coming battle. Patton knew how important it was to keep the objective as the main focus and how easily distraction can occur. This is certainly true today, especially for the believer.

As recorded in Mark 16:15, this was the message, the vision, and the command that our Lord gave His disciples: Preach the gospel to all creation. Obviously, the gospel must have been central to God's plan for His creatures. Following that conclusion, it is also obvious that a clear understanding of the meaning of the gospel becomes critical.

The gospel is the "good news" of what the Creator God has done in giving His Son as a sin offering for fallen man. It tells the story of how God has ransomed for Himself a people, saving them from His just wrath for their sin by permitting His only Son to become a substitute for them. It is the story of the grace of God —that undeserved gift of eternal life; the mercy of God—that pardons from the wrath of God, which we deserve for our sins. It is also the story of the love of

God—the love that is demonstrated by the gift of all good things from above.

The gospel is the very center of the "whole counsel of God." It is the great work of the three persons of the Trinity. It also portrays that part of the character of God that is holy and just and must punish sin but, at the same time, is loving and merciful and desires fellowship with IIis creatures.

Ultimately, it is the gospel of God that overcomes the evil of this present world and the rejection of God by lost sinners.

ACTION STEP:

Make an outline of the major points of the gospel message and use a concordance to locate the appropriate Scripture verses that best relate to each point so you can more easily explain it to others.

FOR FURTHER READING:

Faith Works: The Gospel According to the Apostles chapter 12, pp. 193–212
John F. MacArthur, Jr.

14

The New Birth

· ✄ ·

Jesus answered and said to him, "Most assuredly, I say to you, unless one is born again, he cannot see the kingdom of God" (John 3:3 NKJV).

One of the sad truths of our day is that we hear so little about "the new birth." Rarely is it discussed and seldom do we hear someone refer to it in a conversation among Christians. This is evident in most of the books we read and music we listen to today. Let me quote from two well-known preachers, one from the 1890s and one from the 1990s.

J. C. Ryle was a great English preacher and writer who lived in the latter part of the 1800s. A quote from his book on the new birth is as follows: "The plain truth is, the vast proportion of professing Christians in the world have nothing whatever of Christianity, except the name."

Alistair Begg is pastor of a large congregation in Cleveland, Ohio. He believes the reason so little is referenced about the new birth is that so many who profess Christianity have never undergone this miracle.

Obviously, these observations suggest a serious problem, one that has eternal consequences. Many might ask, "What is the new birth, how does it occur, and what can I do to have it?"

The new birth is a miraculous, supernatural event that takes a person who is dead in sin and brings him to life in Christ. In a spiritual sense, it is the resurrection of a dead person to life. It is a gift from God that is based on the three miracles of salvation accomplished by Jesus Christ some two thousand years ago. The first miracle was the Incarnation, when the God-man, Jesus Christ, was born into the human race yet remained God and lived a perfect life. The second miracle was the Crucifixion, when He was put to death on the cross to become the sacrifice for the sins of His people. The last miracle was the Resurrection, when Jesus Christ was raised from the dead to demonstrate His victory over sin and death and to declare the acceptance and approval of God the Father for His finished work.

The new birth occurs when the Holy Spirit convicts a person of his sins and leads him to repentance. He becomes a new creation. Never again will he look at sin in the same way. He will strive against it for the rest of his life. He will begin a journey of faith. He will grow in love and obedience—failing at times for sure, but progressing all the same to finish his life in a way that is pleasing to God.

Have you undergone the new birth? The Bible gives us many measurements to help us know if we have been born again. How you think and deal with sin is a good indicator of where you are in this question. This is the most important question you will ever answer. Have you been born again? Be sure you know the answer for certain!

ACTION STEP:

Pray and ask God to help you answer the question of whether you have undergone the new birth. Look up the words "new" and "birth" in a Bible concordance. Write out verses relating to the new birth.

FOR FURTHER READING:

A New Birth
pages 69–105
J. C. Ryle

Section 3

GOD WITH US

15
Eternity

Since you have been raised to new life with Christ, set your sights on the realities of heaven, where Christ sits at God's right hand in the place of honor and power. Let heaven fill your thoughts. Do not think only about things down here on earth. For you died when Christ died, and your real life is hidden with Christ in God (Colossians 3:1–3).

The Bible is full of references to eternity. It gives a clear and unmistakable message that every human being formed by God will spend an eternal existence in one of two places: heaven or hell. Erwin Lutzer, pastor of Moody Church in Chicago, expressed it well when he wrote, "One minute after you slip behind the parted curtain, you will either be enjoying a personal welcome from Christ or catching your first glimpse of gloom as you have never known it. Either way, your future will be irrevocably fixed and eternally unchangeable."

Every one of us is immortal, yet most people give scant thought to this fact. Every other issue of life should pale in comparison to the question of our eternal destiny. Unfortunately, many who begin to investigate life after death search in all the wrong places. Numerous cults and sects, offering false solutions and direction, play on the fear of death. The Bible says explicitly that God has provided the only way to heaven. It is through His only Son, Jesus Christ, and His finished work of redemption on the cross. God has also given His people, through the witness of the Holy Spirit and His Word, the assurance that they are going to heaven.

Everyone needs to be mindful of where he or she will spend eternity. The Bible tells us that heaven will be more wonderful than we can imagine, and that hell will be more awful than our minds could ever comprehend.

There are a multitude of distractions in the times in which we live. These distractions can divert our attention and keep our minds off where we are going to spend eternity. Even believers can get so caught up in the things of this world that they forget we are building for eternity. The Bible says that our roles in heaven are being shaped by what we are doing here on earth. The doctrine of heaven and hell is something every believer should understand and be able to explain.

ACTION STEP:

Reflect on what you currently understand about heaven and hell and compare that with what the Bible states on the issue. Take the time to find out what Scripture says about heaven and hell.

FOR FURTHER READING:

One Minute After You Die: A Preview of Your Final Destination
introduction and chapter 1, pp. 9–28
Erwin Lutzer

16

Worship

Give to the Lord the glory he deserves! Bring your offering and come to worship him. Worship the Lord in all his holy splendor (1 Chronicles 16:29).

One of the most interesting truths about the exercise of worship is that God has so ordered it that we become like the things we worship. Pause for a moment and think about the negative and positive implications of this truth.

On the negative side, consider the rampant worship of idols in our American culture. Success, sex, fame, drugs, pleasure, materialism, intellectualism, leisure, and sports are examples of things that have become idols in our society. The list is endless, and the resulting impact from the worship of these things is devastating. Look around yourself and you can see how America is being transformed into a pagan society. Without question, we do grow to be like the things we worship. The act of false worship brings terrible consequences.

On the positive side, reflect on the results of true worship—worship of the true and living God, worship of the God of the Bible, worship of the Father, the Son, and the Holy Spirit. Regard some of God's attributes and characteristics—love, kindness, tenderness, gentleness, peacefulness, truthfulness, compassion, slowness to anger, forgiveness, and mercy. What a wonderful thought it is that we can be changed into the image of the wonderful God we worship.

Recall someone you know who has walked with God for years and has been an active worshiper. What is that person like? Chances are very good that this person will exhibit some of the same characteristics listed above for God. As a believer being transformed into the likeness of Christ, the type of person you are becoming results from your worship of God.

When your eyes, thoughts, and mind are on idols, you become consumed with them and fail to grow in Christ. Your actions become worldly, your witness for Christ is weakened, and you forsake the peace and joy of a pure conscience. Believers need to guard their hearts and minds in actions of worship. Be sure your worship is based on the truth of the Bible and is guided by the Holy Spirit. True worship requires that we commit all that we are—our emotions, our mind, and, most of all, our will—to the only One worthy of worship: our Lord and our God.

ACTION STEP:

Examine the areas in your life that could become idols and some things that have become idols to you and write them down. Commit to pray specifically for God's help in keeping these areas from becoming idols. Keep a log of your progress.

FOR FURTHER READING:

How to Worship Jesus Christ
introduction and chapters 1 and 2, pp. 11–42
Joseph Carroll

17
Bible Study

· ·⸺✛⸻· ·

Be diligent to present yourself approved to God as a workman who does not need to be ashamed, handling accurately the word of truth (2 Timothy 2:15 NASB).

Paul Little, a best-selling author of apologetics and evangelism, made a profound statement when he said that most of God's will for every believer is clearly spelled out in God's Word, the Bible. God does not fail to provide every one of His children with everything needed in their lives of faith; it is our failure to fully avail ourselves of His provision. This is why Bible study is so essential to growth as a believer. Just as proper nourishment is necessary for the growth of a child, so the Word of God is necessary for the growth of the Christian.

Some key fundamentals need to be understood in order to begin the exercise of Bible study. Reading the Bible and studying the Bible are not generally the same. Reading is part of study, but there is a difference. Reading familiarizes us with topics in the Bible, while studying focuses on a particular section and seeks a more comprehensive explanation to what is being said.

There are basically three steps to good Bible study. The first step to cultivate is observation: What do I see? Pay attention to the details. Be sure you understand who is talking, what any reference points are, and what the facts are. The second step is interpreta-

· · · · ·

tion: What does it mean? Analyze the content of what you are studying and then its context. How do the verses relate to other verses surrounding the passage? Be sure you make comparisons of the text you are studying with other portions of Scripture. The Bible is always the best interpreter of itself. The third step in studying the Bible is application: How does it work for me? To make application you must understand the text, yourself, and where you are in relation to the text. Application should be a continual process in your life.

The Bible is the only source in this world that has indisputable truth. This is why the study of God's Word is the most important discipline of life. It is foundational to living the life God intended for each of us.

ACTION STEP:

Read John 3:1–8 and write out what you observe. Interpret what you think it means, and then ask yourself how it applies to you and to others.

FOR FURTHER READING:

Living by the Book
chapter 4, pp. 34–42
Howard G. Hendricks and William D. Hendricks

18

Time Out with God

· ❧ ·

Be still, and know that I am God (Psalm 46:10 NKJV).

One of the sports I really enjoyed when I was young was football. It is a great game—fast paced, hard-hitting, and with the potential for a player to take part in executing a touchdown play or contributing to a goal-line stand that prevents the other team from scoring. It is also a very demanding sport. The intensity of the game requires that teams regularly ask for "time-outs." Most of the time, this is to rest a moment and have some refreshment. At other times, the time-out is to check the defense or revise a critical play. Time-outs are a key part of the game.

In a similar fashion, believers need a daily time-out. This time-out, however, needs to be with God. As disciples of the Lord, we know that, at best, we continually fall short of how we should live in light of the Cross and what Jesus Christ has accomplished for us. We constantly need to be reminded of our behavior and the need for forgiveness. In this way there are some strong similarities to a sport's "time-out." But a much more important distinction needs to be stressed.

If we are to know the Triune God and enjoy a relationship with Him, it must be done in the Spirit. Our God is spirit and we must worship, communicate, and fellowship with Him in the Spirit. It is essential that

· · · · ·

we take time out to exercise this ultimate priority. In the final analysis of life, what matters most will be the time we have spent with our Creator God during our lives on this earth.

Getting away from all of life's other distractions is the first step toward this objective. Learning the importance and the impact this exercise can have on every other part of your life is the second step. Developing it into a daily habit is the final step, which will help it become a regular part of your life.

ACTION STEP:

If you are not in the habit of having a daily devotion, make a commitment to give at least ten minutes a day for a "time-out" with God. Test the time and plan that works best for you.

FOR FURTHER READING:

Daily with the King
W. Glyn Evans

19
Talking with God

· ✂ ·

The earnest prayer of a righteous person has great power and wonderful results (James 5:16).

Many people talk to their god regularly. Some call out to their god in times of crisis or times of great sorrow. But only believers can communicate with the true God, the almighty God, the God of the Bible. Only believers are able to approach a thrice-holy God as sinners, because we come under the blood of the Lamb of God, Jesus Christ our Savior. Only believers have the incredible privilege to talk (or to pray, as it is more traditionally labeled) to the God who made the heavens and the earth and maintains everything by His will and His Word. It is imperative that you are certain you have a personal relationship with the true God. You must be sure the object of your talk or prayer is the God of the Bible.

I am amazed at the energy people expend trying to catch even a glimpse of famous personalities, much less the rare opportunity to speak to them. The possibility to enjoy a conversation with them or to have their undivided attention is almost inconceivable. Yet that is just what we believers have—the unlimited access at any time to approach God, to talk with Him, and to be assured that we have His total focus. Even more encouraging is the fact that God understands everything about us. He sees our hearts, recognizes our needs, and knows what is best for us.

Sadly, prayer for the believer is a wonderful resource that is not being used to its fullest potential and impact. It is clear, if you listen to people talk to God, how many of their conversations are misdirected.

After you have made certain you have the right relationship with the God of the Bible, it is important for you to be able to speak properly with Him. The Bible gives us a perfect example and an outline of how we are to commune with God. It is called the Lord's Prayer, found in Matthew 6:9–13:

> Our Father in heaven, may your name be honored.
> May your Kingdom come soon. May your will be
> done here on earth, just as it is in heaven. Give us our
> food for today, and forgive us our sins, just as we
> have forgiven those who have sinned against us. And
> don't let us yield to temptation, but deliver us from
> the evil one.

This prayer shows most clearly that our fellowship with God should be God-centered, not "me"-centered. Above all things, our prayers must bring praise and worship to our God. Next, we bring thanksgiving and confession of our sins. Then we can bring our requests and intercession for others. We must realize that ultimately everything related to talking with God (praying) is to bring glory to God. Even as God answers our prayers, this brings Him glory.

As believers, one of the most difficult areas of consistency in our faithfulness is in the area of private prayer. Yet, in the final analysis, this, along with Bible study, is one of the most critical disciplines we need to achieve. Without prayer, believers will lack one of the true indications of their assurance of salvation. They will miss the peace and joy of fellowship with their God. They will miss the great encouragement that prayer brings, and they will miss the abundance of God's love that He desires to display to them.

ACTION STEP:

Write out a prayer list for yourself. Plan to talk with God (pray) a minimum of ten minutes each day. Keep a checklist to help you build the habit. Review your results after thirty days, then repeat the process. Continue to build a habit of prayer.

FOR FURTHER READING:

Abba Father: The Lord's Pattern for Prayer
pages 11–28
R. Kent Hughes

20
Thinking About God

This Book of the Law shall not depart from your mouth, but you shall meditate in it day and night, that you may observe to do according to all that is written in it. For then you will make your way prosperous, and then you will have good success (Joshua 1:8 NKJV).

I have just finished reading an outstanding book entitled *God Up Close: Learning to Meditate on His Word* by Doug McIntosh. Every believer should read this book, then learn to apply its instructions. There are two quotations from this book that bring real clarity to the subject of thinking about God. The first quotation is from J. I. Packer: "Meditation is a lost art today, and Christian people suffer grievously from their ignorance of the practice." The second is by Doug McIntosh: "Meditation constitutes the single most important activity that any Christian can engage in. Simply put, it works."

In the first quotation, Dr. Packer brings to summary the plight and problem of many believers today: They suffer grievously. The dictionary says the meaning of grievous is "oppressive and characterized by severe pain, suffering, or sorrow." I submit that if a poll were taken of a majority of pastors across the country, this description would be soundly validated. Countless Christians daily function in a defeated condition.

In the second quotation, Pastor McIntosh summarizes the solution to this problem: Meditation on God through His Word is the single most important activity that any believer can do. Meditation on God through His Word! It is so simple and makes so much sense, and as you begin to practice it you will discover that it works. Your life will be transformed as you enjoy the wonderful pleasure of coming close to God.

Meditation is the believer's means of drawing close to God by reading, studying, and thinking on His Word. It can only be completed by the power of the person of the Holy Spirit, who opens the believer's eyes to the message of Scriptures. As we begin to understand the truths of God, reflect upon those truths, and finally respond to those truths, the process and impact of meditation occurs. As we enjoy this deepened relationship, we come to know more clearly God's will for our lives.

In addition to bringing pleasure to God, meditation provides stability for the believer. God and His Word are sure and they do not change. God alone is faithful and true to everything He has said. Meditation will help you to be contented, producing the peace that is beyond understanding. And meditation will help you become the person God enjoys blessing.

As we pursue the blessing of meditation, there should be one note of caution. In our culture today, there are numerous references to "meditation" that are based on an Eastern religious approach which calls for the emptying of one's mind. Avoid such methods! This is the opposite of biblical meditation, which calls for the filling of the mind with the Word of God. It is the Holy Scriptures that must be the foundation of our meditation, teaching us of the works and ways of God.

It is knowing God, the maker of heaven and earth who sovereignly oversees all things, the God of redemption who transforms lost sinners into His children.

ACTION STEP:

Make a commitment to learn and apply the discipline of biblical meditation. Keep a record of your progress.

FOR FURTHER READING:

God Up Close: Learning to Meditate on His Word
introduction and chapter 1, pp. 2–21
Doug McIntosh

Section 4

A GODLY LIFE

21
Stewardship

. . . . ✢ . . . .

Don't store up treasures here on earth, where they can be eaten by moths and get rusty, and where thieves break in and steal. Store your treasures in heaven, where they will never become moth-eaten or rusty and where they will be safe from thieves. Where your treasure is, there your heart and thoughts will also be (Matthew 6:19–21).

God cares a great deal about the use of money. There is a great deal written in the New Testament about money and our relationship to it. The use of money is a great indicator of one's true profession of faith. Money has tremendous potential to be used for good or for evil. One of the great curses of our society today is materialism—a money-centered and thing-centered focus. Unfortunately, materialism is a big part of everyone's life today, even believers. How we use our money in this life not only affects the time we are here on earth, but it will—as the Bible reinforces—have a profound impact in the life to come.

One of the great battlegrounds for believers is materialism. I am convinced that the bounty of America, which was once a wonderful blessing from God, has now become a curse and judgment from God. We must realize the great danger that materialism poses to our families, our relationships with others, and ultimately our relationships with God. It is essential that we equip ourselves to resist and combat this disastrous sin. The first place to begin is to be certain that we understand and apply this foundational biblical truth:

. . . . .

God owns everything! Nothing I have been provided is mine. God has put me in charge of my time, energy, and money for a limited period to evaluate my decisions on how I use them—for serving myself or for kingdom building. If my choice is to serve myself, then I am investing my treasure where it will be lost, stolen, or corrupted. If my choice is kingdom building, then my treasures will be stored in heaven.

One of the problems with believers today is that we have been strongly influenced to pay more attention to our earthly retirement than to our heavenly retirement. The Bible makes it very clear that how we use our gifts, abilities, time, energy, and money in this life will determine our rewards and roles in heaven. If you think about it, given the short time we live in this life compared with eternity, we should be motivated to spend much more time anticipating and planning for our heavenly retirement.

Some believers think they are free from the sin of materialism because they struggle just to get by and, in their eyes, have very little in the way of material possessions. This can be a dangerous attitude because it is not how much God has given us that determines our eternal outcome, but how faithful we are with what He has given us. There are many who have very little in this life, but who will have mansions in heaven because of their faithfulness.

Good stewardship is one of the foundations of becoming a true disciple of Jesus Christ. All of us need to strive to accomplish this goal in our daily lives. We need to remember that God owns us twice: first because He made us, and second because He redeemed us. We are not our own. All that we have or ever hope to attain belongs to God.

ACTION STEP:

Make a list of the time, energy, and money you invest in kingdom activities. Contrast it with all that you have been given in these areas. Make plans to increase your kingdom investment where necessary.

FOR FURTHER READING:

Money, Possessions and Eternity
chapter 1, pp. 15–29
Randy Alcorn

22

Love

················∞················

Love is patient and kind. Love is not jealous or boastful or proud or rude. Love does not demand its own way. Love is not irritable, and it keeps no record of when it has been wronged (1 Corinthians 13:4–5).

In his best-selling book *The Five Love Languages,* Dr. Gary Chapman develops a clear presentation on the differences between "falling in love" and real love. He points out that "falling in love" is an emotional, instinctive desire to be loved, directed to a large extent at self. Real love, on the other hand, is primarily a willful choice to focus both on our growth and the growth of the one we love. Emotions are involved, but they are balanced with reason. This type of love requires commitment, discipline, and work.

As always, the best place to start to get a proper understanding of what true love is all about is the Word of God. There is one verse, perhaps the greatest single verse in the Bible, that describes a matchless example of God's love: "For God so loved the world that he gave his only Son, so that everyone who believes in him will not perish but have eternal life" (John 3:16). We cannot truly fathom the depth of this illustration of love. It reveals to us that God Himself is, in essence, love.

Another group of verses that allows us a very clear description of true biblical love is found in the thirteenth chapter of First Corinthians. As we read these verses, it soon becomes evident how far short we have fallen from exhibiting true love. It is easy to see why so many marriages and other types of relationships are damaged or destroyed. It is not surprising that the biblical descriptions of love are not what the world advertises. This love takes all that one has to practice it. This love doesn't come easily; it is not natural. As you begin to practice true love, you will see a transformation in yourself as well as in your loved one. True love is foundational to every aspect of our lives. But the dividends are priceless! This is what love was meant to be. This is the love that comes from God, the love that was intended from the beginning.

ACTION STEP:

As you go about your normal routine in the next few weeks, try to make notes of how often "falling in love" instead of real love is the focus in ads, magazines, radio, and television. Also learn which of the five love languages your mate or friend has. The five love languages that are discussed by Dr. Chapman are: words of affirmation, quality time, receiving gifts, acts of service, and physical touch.

FOR FURTHER READING:

The Five Love Languages: How to Express Heartfelt Commitment to Your Mate
chapters 1–3, pp. 11–37
Dr. Gary Chapman

23

Marriage

· ❧ ·

For this reason a man will leave his father and mother and be united to his wife, and they will become one flesh (Genesis 2:24 NIV).

A great tragedy in our day is the breakdown of marriage and the family. Divorce has become commonplace, even among believers. Even when divorce is avoided, an emptiness has replaced the true love that once may have existed in many marriages. Models and examples of wonderful marriages are not easily found, and rarely do you hear resounding testimony to this sacred covenant that God Himself instituted at the beginning of man's existence.

In the second chapter of Genesis, God saw that Adam was alone and had no suitable companion. He planned to create for Adam a complement and a partner. God, in the unity of the Trinity, knew the pleasure of togetherness, so He formed the first marriage in order for Adam and Eve to know the delight of fellowship with one another. Together with God, the first man and woman enjoyed a perfect marriage. Sadly, because of the Fall, this unmarred union was lost and, as with life itself, marriage became a struggle.

When sin and self reign supreme, marriages are destined for failure. For believers, it is possible to regain much of what God intended for the holy covenant of marriage to be. It is possible to enjoy a fulfilling life that leads two different individuals to become one—in mind, in spirit, and in body. Marriage, when Christ is at the center, can be an exciting, fun-filled, rewarding adventure. The real secret to a happy marriage—as in every area of the believer's life—is for both the husband and wife to grow in their likeness to Christ.

Planning, practice, prayer, and a lot of hard work are important principles to remember when building a marriage. At the onset, the couple must determine to stay faithful to each other. They must resolve to accept and keep their vow of "till death do us part." They must practice becoming servants to their mates in the same way Christ was a servant to His disciples. They must learn to lay aside their own self-centeredness. They need to learn to pray together and pray for each other. Finally, they need to work at establishing a marriage that glorifies God.

It is critically important to work at the art of communication. Learn each other's love language. Discover the interests and the temperament of your mate. Avoid taking each other for granted. Keep your interests centered in each other. Don't search for solutions outside your marriage. Build hedges of protection around your home to protect it from the evils of the world and of your own hearts. And, most importantly, submit one to another as unto the Lord. Construct a marriage that witnesses the power of the indwelling Holy Spirit to the world.

ACTION STEP:

Read and review Ephesians chapter five. See the conditions and requirements that are discussed before the commands are given in verses 22–28. Write out the commands that are given in chapter 5 and practice them in your daily life.

FOR FURTHER READING:

Lasting Love
introduction and chapter 1, pp. 13–36
Alistair Begg

24
Family

. . . . ✧ . . . .

So commit yourselves completely to these words of mine. Tie them to your hands as a reminder, and wear them on your forehead. Teach them to your children. Talk about them when you are at home and when you are away on a journey, when you are lying down and when you are getting up again. Write them on the doorposts of your house and on your gates, so that as long as the sky remains above the earth, you and your children may flourish in the land the Lord swore to give your ancestors (Deuteronomy 11:18–21).

On a recent business trip I had the opportunity to visit my hometown. It is good to occasionally visit the place where you grew up because it refreshes memories of your family and the loved ones who played such critical roles in your early development. It enables you to recall earlier times in your life, as well as the scenes when you were a child growing up.

Families are very important to the growth and development of a child—physically, mentally, emotionally, and, most importantly, spiritually. It is no surprise that the Bible states that just as children are a gift from the Lord, families are also a blessing from God. Even for those God has chosen to remain single, being a part of the family of their parents and enjoying the closeness that brings are still important.

Sadly—as with marriage and all other areas of life—sin has taken a hard toll on most families. One of the reasons God hates divorce so much is not only because of what it does to the sacred covenant between the married couple, but because of the impact it has on the children for the rest of their lives (Malachi 2:16). The breakdown of the family over the past fifty years is one of the great tragedies of our society.

As it is in any area of our lives, the key to having a healthy family is to have Christ at the center. It is impossible to have any other enduring relationships in life until one has been restored to a relationship with God, which only comes with the new birth. Only families that are built on the foundation of the Word of God grow and prosper. Only families of believers have any hope of overcoming the influences of the evil of this world.

Unfortunately, there are many believers who are missing out on the blessings the Lord has intended for their families. It is so easy today to be drawn away from the things that strengthen families and to be enticed toward the things the world suggests are most important. Let's review some key points to help build a strong godly family.

First, God should be at the center of everything that takes place in the family and should be viewed as Lord of the family. Second, the marriage is the center point of all families. This is the conventional relationship that God has instituted and formed to protect and expand the family unit. After committing themselves to God, husband and wife must not allow their parents, their own children, or any outside force to compete with or damage their marriage relationship. Third, parents must guard their hearts against influences that draw them away from keeping the Lord's commandments for their family. Fourth, parents need to learn and practice the foundational truths of their faith so they can teach them to their children. Lastly, parents need to model what they teach in their own lives so that their children will see what real faith is and be witness to the transforming power of real Christianity.

As many historians have said, "The family is the building block of society; as the family goes, so goes society." That is the way God designed it. It is our responsibility to do it His way.

_____

ACTION STEP:

Write out a simple mission statement that outlines the priorities that both the husband and wife agree are essential to building a happy, God-centered marriage and family.

_____

FOR FURTHER READING:

Home with a Heart: Encouragement for Families
Dr. James Dobson

25
Relationships

· ❧ ·

Jesus replied, "The most important commandment is this: 'Hear, O Israel! The Lord our God is the one and only Lord. And you must love the Lord your God with all your heart, all your soul, all your mind, and all your strength.' The second is equally important: 'Love your neighbor as yourself.' No other commandment is greater than these" (Mark 12:29–31).

Each Sunday brings with it a wonderful opportunity for every believer to celebrate and deepen his relationship with God and other believers through the act of worship in a church body setting. It is in participating in this important act that we learn to fulfill the two greatest commandments as spoken by our Lord in the twelfth chapter of Mark's gospel: "Love the Lord your God with all your heart, soul, mind, and strength, and your neighbor as yourself." Through the act of worship, the believer has the opportunity to focus on strengthening this relationship through songs, prayer, confession, and learning the Word of God. It should be our platform to begin each new week, impacting our conduct toward God and toward our neighbors.

Proper worship should usher the believer into a special time in the presence of God and guide him in the direction of thanksgiving, repentance, and holy living. It is a time to listen to God and to what He has said to us through His Word. It is a time to look at ourselves in light of that Word and to confront and confess our sins. This is a time when we can sing praises to Him

· · · · ·

and thank Him for what He has done for us. And it is this vital time that marks just how we will live and conduct ourselves in the coming week.

Another blessing of strengthening our intimacy with God is the effect it has on the entire family. As husband and wife come closer to the Lord, they become closer to each other. As families worship together, they are nourished by the experience and their foundation as a unit is made firm. Their relationship to each other is fortified and they learn how to live godly lives together in acceptance and love. They hear God's commandments and seek to apply these truths with one another.

As we grow in the Lord and mature in our understanding of His Word, we become better neighbors to those around us. And as we become better neighbors, people God has placed in our lives are drawn to Christ. This is one of the main channels God has been pleased to use to expand His kingdom.

As I've discussed in earlier topics, it is one's proper relationship with God that has the greatest impact on all other relationships in life. Failure at this juncture is where many believers begin the gradual decline that affects every other area of their lives. This is why many Christian marriages end in divorce and why their families sometimes mirror the troubled and unsaved families around them. The Bible makes it very clear: Apart from Christ, we can do nothing positive for the kingdom. But through Christ, we can have relationships with our mates that glorify and bring pleasure to God. We can have solid relationships with our

children, and we can effectively reach out to our
neighbors and serve those around us.

_____

ACTION STEP:

*Be sure you and your family are active in a solid,
Bible-teaching church. Then think of ways you can
better prepare for your weekly worship time with the
Lord. Make a commitment to grow in your relationship with God and with others.*

_____

FOR FURTHER READING:

The Pursuit of God
A. W. Tozer

26
Sharing Your Faith

· ✣ ·

Always be prepared to give an answer to everyone who asks you to give the reason for the hope that you have (1 Peter 3:15 NIV).

Most of us would agree that it is frustrating to stop and ask someone for directions to a specific destination, only to find out from that person's response that they aren't sure how to get there themselves. Even worse are those situations when the person seems convincing and definitive in giving the directions but turns out to be totally wrong. Unfortunately, many people seek directions in life situations but receive confusing and incorrect answers. Those answers often come from those of us who are supposed to have the directions. Sadly, many believers are not prepared to give a sound reason when someone asks why they have the hope of eternal life. Tragically, there are countless individuals willing and eager to provide people with directions that are totally wrong.

As children of God, we have been called to be prepared to share our faith and point the lost to Jesus Christ. In order to do that with clarity, accuracy, and compassion, we must be growing in our own understanding of God's Word and in our personal relationship with Christ. The believer who is not growing is fading. This is one of the compelling motives for my writing this book. All believers need to be maturing

· · · · ·

daily in their walk with the Lord and deepening the knowledge of their faith.

As our minds and hearts are properly prepared to explain the hope that is within us, we should examine our own families and circle of friends to see if there may be a need for some of them to come to Christ. Begin by praying for those relationships and asking God for the opportunity to discuss the issue of eternity with those people. Take time to get to know how others are thinking about this topic of eternity. Seek ways to engage them in conversations that invite your telling the truth from the Word of God. Always speak the truth in love. Avoid confrontational discussions and never force involvement if they do not invite dialog.

Believers must always remember that the Holy Spirit does the work of preparation as well as the work of bringing a person to saving faith (regeneration). It is our role to be willing and able to provide the gospel message and be ready to provide biblical answers to questions they may want to ask.

It is also important to remember that in many ways it will be the testimony of how we live daily that causes others to notice a real difference in our lives as compared with those of nonbelievers. This is why it is so critical for us to be in constant fellowship with the Lord and have a clear understanding of His Word—that our lives may reflect Him to others. Strive to always be prepared.

ACTION STEP:

Take time to think about your personal testimony. Ask yourself if you can present a clear presentation of the gospel and what the basics of the Christian faith are all about. If you find that you are not able to do that, then prepare yourself through prayer and through the study of the Word.

FOR FURTHER READING:

Explaining Your Faith
introduction, pp. 11–19
Alister McGrath

Section 5

AN ORGANIZED LIFE

27

Getting Started

Whatever your hand finds to do, do it with all your might, for in the grave, where you are going, there is neither working nor planning nor knowledge nor wisdom (Ecclesiastes 9:10 NIV).

The first habit of highly successful people is that of being proactive, which is another way of saying "getting started." Successful people know how to get started, whatever the objective. Many people think about getting started but never do. Others talk a lot about getting started but seldom do. Some plan to get started but never get past their plans. Fear and doubt keep many from getting started. Lack of focus has stopped numerous well-intentioned people. There are countless ways to avoid getting started, yet it is only by getting started that anything is ever accomplished.

How do some manage to start when multitudes generally don't? Are there any effective approaches to help one begin something? How can I learn to get started? There are some fundamentals that will help the believer in Jesus Christ get started. One of the most important verses to learn is Matthew 6:33: "But seek first the kingdom of God and His righteousness, and all these things shall be added to you" (NKJV).

Getting started in the right direction is the most important element of starting. To do that, you must be earnest about seeking Christ and His kingdom. Become proactive. Get serious with where you are in life and with what you are doing. Grow where you are planted. Pray for guidance, strength, boldness, wisdom, and patience. Work, strive, push, learn, START. Take the first step and keep it up. Just do it! Learn, learn, learn! Each element will begin to make a difference. Concentrate on the most important basics and choose one you can begin. Do things you enjoy. Do things with others. Make a game out of getting started and keep a record of your victories. Remember to begin with small goals or objectives and build off those. Make a commitment to war against procrastination. Stop putting off things. Plan to start, then DO IT!

ACTION STEP:

Write down three things you will commit to starting in the coming month. Three good suggestions might be to (1) pray for five minutes every day; (2) read one chapter of the Bible daily; and (3) read one devotional every day. Be sure to do it; don't put it off.

FOR FURTHER READING:

Spiritual Disciplines for the Christian Life
chapter 2, pp. 23–35
Donald S. Whitney

28
Developing Good Habits

. . . . ✂ . . . .

But when Daniel learned that the law had been signed, he went home and knelt down as usual in his upstairs room, with its windows open toward Jerusalem. He prayed three times a day, just as he had always done, giving thanks to his God (Daniel 6:10).

One of the best-selling books of this decade, *Seven Habits of Highly Effective People,* analyzes seven practices that are characteristic of outstanding, successful people. These habits are very sound and can no doubt improve anyone's daily routine. Developing good habits is one of the foundational qualities of life that everyone should strive to acquire. Good habits continually produce positive results, whereas bad habits weaken the best of efforts.

The pursuit of establishing desirable habits begins by drawing from the best source for all wisdom and truth, the Bible. The book of Proverbs is particularly applicable to this objective. Proverbs was written especially for young people—or for those still young in their faith—but it seems that the older we get, the more relevant it becomes. These wonderful, wise words should be read daily by both young and old. The book of Proverbs deals at length with the subject of wisdom or skillfulness. Both of these terms mean the ability to use knowledge correctly. Proverbs also tells us where the beginning of knowledge lies: "Fear of the Lord is the beginning of knowledge. Only fools despise wisdom and discipline" (Proverbs 1:7). There

. . . . .

should be no doubt that this is the right place to begin our search.

After knowing the right source for knowledge, wisdom, and truth comes the process of learning how to assimilate this information and instruction into habits of life. Many have said that if you do something for twenty-one days, it will then become a habit. I am inclined to believe that, given the impressions that bombard our minds, it is better to think in terms of one month, or thirty days. A monthly goal is easier to measure. The critical point is that the time period must be "uninterrupted." If there is any break in the thirty days, you need to start over.

Additionally, you need to begin with the end in mind and keep your focus on the goal. This will help motivate you and keep you away from preoccupation with the practice or execution of the discipline you are working on. Contemplate how satisfied you are going to be when you have developed this habit. Weigh the positive benefits against the negative habit you are replacing.

One last thing—if you at first don't succeed, try, try, try again. Stick to your goal. Continue to ask God to help you. Eventually you will succeed. After you learn the art of developing good habits, the discipline of the process will work even better with each new effort.

ACTION STEP:

Make a commitment to read one chapter in the book of Proverbs every day. Pray and ask God to help you apply the book as you establish good habits in your life.

FOR FURTHER READING:

Choices for a Lifetime
chapters 1 and 2, pp. 1–20
Stuart Briscoe

29
The Little Things

......................✕......................

His master replied, "Well done, good and faithful servant! You have been faithful with a few things; I will put you in charge of many things" (Matthew 25:21 NIV).

It has been forty years since I obtained my first driver's license. It was about that same time I received a valuable lesson—a "little thing" that has paid dividends all my life. My dad taught me the value of changing the oil in a car regularly. He explained that this procedure, although it isn't noticeable when you look at a car from the outside, would have a greater impact over the long run than almost anything else related to servicing a car.

Life has a lot of "little things" that have important consequences. Here are a few I have learned during the past forty-something years:

By far, the most important "little thing" is the need to read your Bible every day—even if it's only for ten minutes. Over time, it will have greater influence on you than everything else combined. Also, learn to use five little words that will make a real difference in all areas of your life: "Please," "Thank you," and "I'm sorry." Develop the habit of listening—a "little thing" that can transform how you relate to other people. Make a concerted effort to do "little things" for others. The impact will be amazing. Remember to rest on Sunday; it will have a tremendous influence on the other six days of the week. Determine to learn something new every day. The "little things" of learning add up to rewarding results. Make a habit of writing down things every day. Writing down your thoughts, ideas, and objectives is another way to improve in the "little things." Be sure to keep a written prayer list and pray for others. It will reap wonderful benefits. Always remember that the "little things" add up. Over time they become part of the main thing. Be mindful of the "little things." Practice them and watch how they affect your life.

ACTION STEP:

Review the list of "little things" I have mentioned above and start a list of your own. Begin to practice those things each day. Keep a checklist of your progress for the next month, continuing to add to your list as you see how the "little things" can enrich your life.

FOR FURTHER READING:

Life's Little Instruction Book: 511 Suggestions, Observations, and Reminders on How to Live a Happy and Rewarding Life
H. Jackson Brown, Jr.

30
Discipline

⸎

Train yourself to be godly (1 Timothy 4:7 NIV).

One of the most profitable books I have ever read is *Disciplines of a Godly Man* by R. Kent Hughes. In it, the author makes two statements I believe hold some of life's most profound truths, truths that can have a great practical impact on our lives. He states: "God has so ordered that personal discipline is the indispensable key for accomplishing anything in this life," and, "We will never get anywhere in life without discipline, be it in business, athletics, or academics. This is doubly so in spiritual matters."

The dictionary defines discipline as the "training that corrects, molds, or perfects the mental faculties and the moral character." In other words, learn the correct way of doing something and develop it by practice. Learn to do the right thing in the right way. Repeat the process until it becomes a natural part of how you do things. Developing discipline requires focus, commitment, and time, and it takes work. But until the practice of discipline is mastered, progress in every area of your life will produce less than pleasing results.

As you grow in the knowledge and understanding of God's truth from His Word, you begin to appropriate these truths into your daily life. The discipline toward godliness is foundational. Without this, your life will never be what God intends it to be. The Bible continually calls believers to a life of discipline for the purpose of godliness.

One secret to developing a discipline in any area is to be honest in admitting your shortcomings. Next, lay out an objective to make small improvements. Learn ways to make it easier; employ tools that help you accomplish your goals. Above all, work at it. If you fail, try again. Be diligent, and eventually you will make progress. Consistency is the essential factor in becoming disciplined.

One reminder: Discipline is critical to growth, but dependency is the other side of the coin. Discipline is important, but we must continue to depend on the Holy Spirit to achieve any and all spiritual growth. It is by obedience to God's commandments and instructions, led by the Holy Spirit, that we are able to apply the energy to become disciplined.

ACTION STEP:

Ask God to help you focus on one area where you can become more disciplined. It may be in the area of daily Bible reading. Make a commitment to become disciplined in this area.

FOR FURTHER READING:

Disciplines of a Godly Man
introduction, pp. 13–19
R. Kent Hughes

31
Focus

····························· ❧ ·····························

Look straight ahead, and fix your eyes on what lies
before you. Mark out a straight path for your feet; then
stick to the path and stay safe (Proverbs 4:25–26).

One of my favorite old movies is *Sergeant York,* star-
ring Gary Cooper. It is based on the life of Alvin C.
York, America's greatest hero from World War I. It
depicts a wonderful story of the impact of the Lord
Jesus Christ in the life of a lost soul. The movie also
provides a classic example of the power of focus.

Alvin York was born into a poor family who farmed
the "poor ground" on the upper slopes in the moun-
tains of Tennessee. Alvin's desire was to buy some of
the rich-soiled "bottom land" so he could become a
successful farmer. Alvin demonstrated the results that
can be achieved when one becomes focused. His every
waking moment was directed at getting that "bottom
land." He accomplished unbelievable results because
of his intense concentration on his goal.

Even though Alvin raised enough money to buy the
land he wanted, the owner sold it to someone else—
just another reminder that God is sovereign and con-
trols the outcome of all things. Eventually, after the
war, Sergeant York received that rich land. It was a
gift from the grateful and proud people of his native
state of Tennessee and a wonderful reminder of God's
goodness to a faithful servant.

····

Another example of the powerful impact of focus can be seen in the lives of athletes. The discipline of powerful concentration aimed at a clear objective produces amazing results. Unfortunately, that degree of focus is not easily attained. It takes initiative and it takes practice. This is especially true in regard to the believer's focus on the Word of God. As believers our greatest area of focus should be on the Lord Jesus Christ and the Word of God. Psalm 119 reminds us of the need to establish our thoughts on God's Word. The psalmist prays for his eyes to be "opened" and "fixed" upon God's laws; he speaks of meditating and reflecting, of setting his heart and hiding God's Word in his heart. When we fail to saturate our hearts with God's Word, it affects every area of our lives. Nothing is more important than staying focused on the Word of God. To mature in Christ, we must become more and more familiar with what God is saying to us through His Word. When our hearts are focused on God, our lives are filled with meaningful purpose.

ACTION STEP:

Psalm 119 consists of twenty-two sections arranged according to the Hebrew alphabet. Take one section of this psalm and make a list of the ways the psalmist tells us of the importance of focusing on God's Word. Review this list regularly. Example—HE (the fifth letter): Teach me. Give me understanding. Make me walk. Incline my heart. Turn away my eyes. Establish Your Word. Revive me.

FOR FURTHER READING:

Sgt. York: His Life, Legend & Legacy
chapters 1 and 2, pp. 1–32
John Perry

32
Gifts and Abilities

. . . . ·⚭· . . . .

God has given gifts to each of you from his great variety of spiritual gifts. Manage them well so that God's generosity can flow through you (1 Peter 4:10).

In some areas of learning, it has taken me a lot of hard work and time just to reach an acceptable level of accomplishment. Yet in other places, the effort was not so demanding but came quite naturally to me. There are also certain areas, such as playing a musical instrument or singing, where I have no talent or ability at all. So it is with most people—some things are easier to grasp than others. God has given everyone gifts and abilities. Gifts are those areas of natural talent and inclination that can produce extraordinary achievement if they are developed. There are varying degrees of giftedness.

Aptitude is the natural ability that allows us to effectively learn and develop the skills necessary to be successful in the area of our calling. The willingness to learn, to try new things, and to be persistent all play roles in how we develop those gifts and abilities.

Unfortunately, many people never discover God's purpose for their lives and do not recognize the wonderful gifts He has given them. Consequently, their talents are never used. For some people, this is because they grew up in circumstances where little or no encouragement was offered. This environment can be a breeding ground for discouragement. Many children grow up

. . . . .

being told what they should be like instead of being given the motivation to discover how God made them. Some people never properly utilize their gifts because of wrong motivations. Materialism and love of money influence some people to pursue the wrong vocation. Others become so engrossed in what they are doing that they never see their potential.

It is sad to see so many people who are unfulfilled, who don't enjoy what they do for a living, and who fail to reach their maximum potential. This is one reason why so many people are tempted to get involved with foolish pursuits that only end in failure. Unsettled, unfulfilled, and unhappy people are always targets for exploitation from unscrupulous characters.

God intends that we as His children strive to recognize the gifts and abilities He has given us in order that we might grow to effectively use them for His glory. Only then can we fulfill the desires of our hearts and accomplish our roles in this life. We have been given the Holy Spirit, who longs to lead us in the direction of our inherent tendencies. He also plays a role in helping us recognize our spiritual gifts, which only believers are given for the building of Christ's church and the edification of fellow believers.

God can use family, friends, and coworkers to provide valuable input and encouragement related to our gifts and abilities. Most importantly, we need to continue to learn to understand ourselves as God has made us and seek to do His will for our lives.

ACTION STEP:

Set a goal to ask ten people you know—coworkers, people from your church, or your close friends—to give you input on what they see as your strengths and abilities. Match this information with your own assessment, and think about how this input can help direct you in your work.

FOR FURTHER READING:

Finding the Career That Fits You
chapter 3, pp. 29–68 (including personality profile analysis)
Lee Ellis and Larry Burkett

A Calling

······················· ✂ ·······················

God has given each of us the ability to do certain things well (Romans 12:6 NLT).

It has now been more than seventeen years since one of the most traumatic events of my life. Soon after I came to a saving faith in the Lord Jesus Christ, God made it very clear to me that He wanted me to give up my very successful career of twelve years in the medical-health industry and chart a new course in life. He chose not to reveal the direction to me at that point. By God's grace and by faith, my family and I embarked on what would become an experience that only a child of God can know. These were years of hardship, disappointment, and discouragement, as well as times of growing, learning, and rejoicing. During those years, God was working out His calling in our lives.

Today, and over the past few years, I have been blessed with the wonderful assurance of knowing I am exactly where God intended me to be. I sense His pleasure in my fulfilling what He has given me to do. I think about God's faithfulness regularly and long for others to know the joy and excitement that comes from acknowledging their calling. I pray the example of my background might be helpful to others.

Let's define what a biblical calling is. It starts with God's purpose for all those He has called to repentance and faith in the Lord Jesus Christ. He has ordained a mission and a role for each of His children in the building of His kingdom. This mission may or may not be known by the believer at the beginning of the Christian life, or sometimes for years. Our calling is defined by the gifts and abilities God has given each of us, the confirmation of others, and the desires and circumstances that God allows in our lives.

Every one of God's children has a calling. Some, like myself, have realized that wonderful place where gifts, desires, and abilities fit so well with what God has called them to do. Others are still discovering where God wants them to be. Some are in the midst of struggles because they are still aspiring to be what they want to be rather than what God wants. Some might feel satisfied with where they are in life but sense that something is missing. This may well be a case when someone is "successful in the world's eyes," but who, in reality, has missed his or her calling.

In seeking your calling, first be sure you are in the right relationship with God. Many go through life not understanding their real standing before God. This can give them a false sense of who they really are and a flawed foundation from which to find their true calling. Make sure your life is consistent with a biblical understanding of what the clear signs of a new birth in Christ are.

Evaluate what your gifts and abilities are and think about what you enjoy doing. What things in your life have been confirmed by others? Where has God placed you? What education, training, or experiences have you had? All of these elements will help you toward realizing your calling. The most important thing is to spend more time with God—in His Word and in prayer and conversation with Him. The rewards of knowing your calling will be immeasurable.

ACTION STEP:

Take time to think about what you would most like to do and about what you sense God has called you to do. If you are not doing it right now, ask friends how you might develop an approach to make a change in your vocation.

FOR FURTHER READING:

A Case for Calling
Dr. Thomas Addington and Dr. Stephen Graves

Section 6

A FOCUSED LIFE

34

A Mission Statement

......................✂......................

Above all else, guard your heart, for it affects everything you do (Proverbs 4:23).

I am sure every adult has had at least one person tell him or her, "You ought to have a will." Everyone should have a will.

It is somewhat the same with a mission statement. Yes, there are some differences, but as a person begins to understand the lasting impact a mission statement can have on his or her life, the similarities will be more recognizable. Everyone should develop a mission statement.

Just what is a mission statement? It is a summary account reflecting the foundational principles and truths of your life, the core values of your beliefs, and the vision of what you desire to fulfill for your life.

A mission statement needs to be reviewed regularly. Why? Because a mission statement serves as the overarching master plan for your life. It represents the dominant benchmark for use in every area of your existence. It is the overall paradigm through which you process decisions. It will serve to keep you on target. It should serve as the foundation for all phases of your planning.

How can you develop a mission statement? First, begin by thinking about the thoughts and principles by which you operate. Do you believe God has a specific plan for your life? What gifts and abilities do you recognize in yourself? Second, ask yourself what circumstances of life have brought you to where you are now. Where has God placed you? Are you being fulfilled? Third, think about the responsibilities with which you have been entrusted. Are you married? Do you have children? What about your career? Fourth, think about your vision of how these areas fit together. Where do you want to be in three, five, and ten years? What kind of person do you want to become? What are the real priorities of your life?

As you answer these questions, your mission statement will begin to take shape. In most cases it takes a number of drafts to reach an acceptable statement. Over time your mission statement may change. The real key is to go through the process of its development.

ACTION STEP:

Make a list of the most important things in your life. Make another list of the things you believe (not what you say you believe, but what you live out). After you have taken these steps, do a first draft of your mission statement. Keep it simple at first. Here is an example of a style you might use. The important thing is to commit your mission statement to writing.

MY MISSION STATEMENT (an example)
1. *I want to keep God at the center of every area of my life.*
2. *I want to continue to grow as a believer in Christ through a commitment to study and apply God's Word.*

3. *I want to be the respectful and loving husband/wife that God commands me to be.*
4. *I want to be a godly parent for my children.*
5. *I want my life to show Christ in my workplace.*
6. *I want to use my gifts and abilities for God's kingdom, starting with service in my church.*
7. *I want to be a witness for Christ in my neighborhood.*
8. *I want to be a good steward of my time and possessions.*

FOR FURTHER READING:

Living the Life You Were Meant to Live
chapters 1 and 2, pp. 1–28
Tom Paterson

35

Life Goals

❧

So our aim is to please him always (2 Corinthians 5:9).

A truly distinct blessing of growing older in life is the gift of grandchildren. One of the unquestionable joys of my life is our four-year-old grandson, Stephen. In just four short years he has captured the hearts of his adoring "Opa" and "Oma." We look with anticipation at every opportunity to spend time with him and see him grow and develop. Like most grandparents, we give much thought and prayer to the type of person he will grow to become. The greatest hope and desire of our hearts is that he will someday come to a saving faith in the Lord Jesus Christ and that he will make as his primary "life goal" to be pleasing to the Lord in all the areas of his life.

There can be no greater life goal than that of dedicating our lives to service that is pleasing to the Lord of Glory. This must be the foundational platform from which all other life goals emanate and point toward. Unfortunately, since we live in a world so preoccupied with self, it is very easy, even as believers, to be drawn away from what should be our primary objective in life. Pleasing God ought to be manifest in every aspect of our existence. Our whole being should be exercised in order to please God. We need to learn that we can give God great pleasure in the simple things of life when we do them to and for His glory.

God has created in each of us a wonderful array of talents, gifts, and abilities. He has provided us countless environments and influences and has implanted within each of us a rainbow of interests and fascinations. These endowments are from our Creator, and as we better understand ourselves, our children, and our grandchildren, we begin to see some other life goals taking shape. It is important to cultivate and respond to these areas in ourselves and in those around us. It is also critical that we view them in light of our primary life goal of pleasing Him. This will be a guiding element in all the other life goals we set for ourselves.

Planning life goals is a very important exercise. Life is short, and it is easy to get caught up in the business of the moment and miss out on what you were meant to be and do for the kingdom. If you have never really thought about life goals, you can start now. You may already be doing what is most important in setting life goals to some degree: pleasing God. Remember to ask God for help in directing and opening doors to confirm your life goals. Be patient and watchful. The life of a believer can be exciting and wonderful.

ACTION STEP:

Write down five of the most important things you want to do before you are called home to heaven. List five things you can improve in the area of pleasing God every day. Commit your goals to prayer. Periodi-

cally review both of your lists and watch for ways that will help you cultivate both.

As you begin to think about developing a life goal for yourself, it might be helpful to have an example. The following is my life goal, which has taken many years to formulate and may well be modified or expanded in the future.

The Life Goal of William L. Thrasher, Jr.

My life goal is to know and love the Triune God, to serve Him in a way that brings Him pleasure and contributes to His kingdom. I seek to fulfill this goal by learning to live a godly life, and through the writing and publishing of biblically centered materials as my vocational calling.

FOR FURTHER READING:

Made for His Pleasure
introduction and chapter 1, pp. 15–42
Alistair Begg

36

Goal Setting

· ∞ ·

Show me the path where I should walk, O Lord; point out the right road for me to follow (Psalm 25:4).

One of the lies of Satan that constantly influences nonbelievers is that once you become a Christian you will lose your freedom to choose and be forced into a rigid, confining lifestyle. However, as believers can affirm, just the opposite takes place. The Bible tells us that the only real freedom apart from Christ is the freedom to sin. Every thought, every plan, every desire, every goal the unbeliever has is swayed by and, in many cases, dominated by sin. In truth, the nonbeliever is in bondage—in his thoughts, his actions, and even his plans.

In contrast, it is actually believers who have real liberty because they are acquainted with the truth. We are blessed with the presence of the third person of the Trinity, the Holy Spirit, who lives within us. His responsibility is to guide, teach, and direct our plans and objectives in life. One area where He assumes this role is in helping us to establish and then achieve goals in our lives.

Setting goals is a discipline whereby we determine the results we want to accomplish in specific areas of our lives. For the believer, it should always start with the spiritual life, since that is the essence of who we are in Christ. It also involves marriage, family life, church life, areas of finance and profession, as well as the physical and recreational aspects of our routines. Dreaming the way things could be in all of these areas is the beginning of goal setting.

The next step is to capture those dreams in writing and organize them by the specific areas: spiritual, marriage, family, church, professional, financial, and physical. It is important to remember to keep your goals specific, realistic, and reasonable in terms of the time required to accomplish them. As you develop this discipline you may want to divide your goal setting into short-, medium-, and long-term objectives. This categorizing can be very helpful as you become more effective in the use of this skill.

A very important point to remember in the practice of goal setting is that goals are changeable. As we grow and mature, we learn more and more about ourselves and our gifts and abilities. More than anything else, we begin to uncover the depths of who we are in Christ, the purpose for which God has created us (for His glory and service), and the true desires of our heart. This is a gradual process that takes time, but as we work out our salvation by the leading of the Holy Spirit, the journey becomes more and more exciting.

Goal setting is critical to a life well lived for Christ and His kingdom. Organizing your dreams is not hard; it just takes time and practice. Eventually you will see how distinct your goals become. You will know the joy of accomplishment in realizing those goals.

ACTION STEP:

Take a sheet of paper and make a list of the seven sections of life mentioned. Then list one result for each area you would like to accomplish. Keep it simple, precise and to the point.

FOR FURTHER READING:

Nine Empowering Secrets of Successful Living introduction and chapter 1, pp. v–35
Denis Waitley

37

Planning

. . . . ✂ . . . .

The wisdom of the prudent is to give thought to their ways (Proverbs 14:8 NIV).

Planning, like most things in life, improves as you do it more. Almost everyone plans, even though a great deal of planning is done without much real thought. If a person is serious about seeing positive results in areas of his life, good planning is essential.

Most people approach planning incorrectly, and therefore they come to the conclusion that planning is too complicated, or that planning is not critical to what they want to accomplish. Both of these conclusions are erroneous.

An excellent way to learn the art of planning is to approach the process in much the same way you learned to read. When you began to learn to read, you started with the ABC's. After that, you learned to form words from those letters, then you learned to read simple sentences. Finally, you learned to read whole pages of words.

In the ABCs of planning, there are also three basic steps. The first is to always record your plans in writing. Something not written down is too easily lost. Second, be brief and to the point in everything you write. This is critical in both the writing and in reviewing what you have written. And third, check off or clear out what has been accomplished and continue what still needs to be done.

The first steps in planning are to mentally commit to learning to plan better. Next, decide what type of planning tools best complement you and your circumstances. (See appendix A, "Tools for the Journey.") Remember to keep it simple and build from there.

As you progress with the ABCs of planning, you will begin to see the value and positive impact planning produces. Moving from daily, weekly, and monthly planning, you will begin to develop longer-range planning. You will also begin to form plans related to specific goals or projects. As planning becomes a habit, you will discover that you grow more and more proficient in the process. And remember, every action of a believer should be approached with prayer.

ACTION STEP:

Select one area where you are going to start to plan. Spend some time to work out goals and a timetable. Commit your plans to writing with appropriate checkpoints on your progress.

FOR FURTHER READING:

Timing Is Everything
chapters 1–3, pp. 1–24
Denis Waitley

38
Work

· ✂ ·

Then the Lord God took the man and put him into the garden of Eden to cultivate it and keep it (Genesis 2:15 NASB).

Work was one of the first blessings as well as one of the first responsibilities God gave to man. A majority of people today would probably question "work and blessing" being applied together, but work was created and ordered from God to provide Adam and Eve with purpose and pleasure in activities that were pleasing to God (cultivating and keeping the garden).

Work is a demonstration of our being created in the likeness of God, for work requires vision, thought, and purpose. Our Creator God provided an outstanding example of work in His creation of the heavens and the earth. On the sixth day He reviewed the work He had accomplished and was very pleased. God demonstrated that He honored work because He Himself worked.

As believers, we need to realize that we are coworkers with God. Each of us has a "calling." God has given each of us gifts and abilities that are intended to be used to further the purposes that He has ordered for all of His creation. We will better comprehend the dignity, value, and worth of work as we better define what God has called us to do and gifted us for in our areas of work. The satisfaction that comes from fulfilling the role we have been called to do in God's king-

· · · · ·

dom will grow as we mature in our faith and obedience to His will for our lives.

Work in whatever area for which we have been equipped is one of the ways we serve and please God, in addition to serving the needs of ourselves and others. There are many obstacles against achieving the work God has purposed for each and every one of us. The most monumental obstruction is sin, which has impaired everything, including mankind and his environment. Yet even under these circumstances, through a better understanding of who we are and what God desires of us, we can enjoy work as a wonderful gift from God.

ACTION STEP:

Make a list of what you believe are your strengths and areas of giftedness. Ask yourself if these are being used in your current work. If not, think about ways this may become possible.

FOR FURTHER READING:

Your Work Matters to God
chapter 1, pp. 13–24
Doug Sherman and William Hendricks

39
Leisure

·· ✂ ··

On the seventh day, having finished his task, God rested
from all his work. And God blessed the seventh day and
declared it holy, because it was the day when he rested
from his work of creation (Genesis 2:2–3).

There are few things in this day and age on which
most people would agree, but I submit that leisure is
something that would win almost universal endorse-
ment. Everyone, even the workaholic, loves leisure
time. Leisure is the main theme of many people's lives.
Most of their time is spent on planning and preparing
for times of relaxation. The industry to support the
tools and toys of leisure is mammoth. For many, the
majority of time off from their work environment is
consumed with this one passion. Leisure is not only a
favorite topic for many, but their favorite activity.
Some, unfortunately, are consumed by the desire for
leisure.

The Bible tells us that God created leisure (another
word for rest, meaning the time set aside from work or
duties) for people. Just as He had done with work,
God established rest or leisure before the Fall. These
activities were kept in balance, and both were blessings from the Lord. God initiated leisure for the benefit of mankind because He knew it would be beneficial
and needed. Much of human history contains evidence
that leisure was not enjoyed much at all. For centuries,
the blessing of rest was only a dream reserved for an
elite few. Over the past hundred years, however,

leisure has become increasingly more accessible for the majority of people, especially in the developed nations of the world.

Like work, leisure can become very harmful if not kept within the proper perspective. God has made it evident that He wants everyone to enjoy times of leisure. The problem begins when believers forget the other part of leisure—that "rest beyond leisure," which Gordon MacDonald writes about in his book, *Ordering Your Private World*. God set this pattern from the beginning: Human beings need a time to rest and an extended time to fellowship with God. When this combination of respite and relationship with Him does not occur, the believer is subject to physical weakness as well as spiritual vulnerability.

For the believer, Sunday, the first day of the week, is our day of rest and leisure. We should learn to use this day primarily for the purposes God intended: for our well-being. If possible, every Sunday should be viewed as an extended time to worship, reflect on, and appreciate the wonderful God we worship. It is also a time to review the priorities in our lives. It is a time to ask if we have really pleased God during the past week or have been drawn toward the things of this world. It should be used as an occasion to think about the real purposes of life and to redirect ourselves to the things that truly matter.

Learning to handle leisure time and to make certain we keep the right priorities on Sunday will go a long way toward the growth of the believer.

ACTION STEP:

Review how much time you spend engaged with God every Sunday. Make a commitment to use this time to really rest and fellowship with God.

FOR FURTHER READING:

Ordering Your Private World (Expanded Edition) chapter 14, pp. 173–88
Gordon MacDonald

40

Time Management

· ∞ ·

Be very careful, then, how you live—not as unwise but as wise, making the most of every opportunity (Ephesians 5:15–16 NIV).

A common riddle most of us are very familiar with goes like this: "What is something everyone has the same amount of and that in no way can any be added to or subtracted from but is fixed for all of one's life?" The answer is the twenty-four hours that make up each and every day. As long as you live, there will never be more or less than twenty-four hours contained in a single day. With that in mind, it is easy to see why time management has become such a hot subject. Actually, a much better label would be "management of the uses of time." We really can only manage how we use time, not time itself.

One of the first steps in better managing one's use of time is to review how you currently use your time. When most people do this, they are surprised to learn how much of their day is actually wasted. In most cases, it is not planned. It just happens, and that is a big part of the problem. It is alarming when you think about how much time you squander over the course of a year.

What, then, can be done to improve the use of that precious commodity we call time? Once you realize how much time you waste, attempt to alter bad time-use habits you have developed. Write down how you

· · · · ·

use your time. Start the process of planning the use of your time, but leave some totally free time. Learn to spot "time wasters"–things that use up time with very little results to show for it. Guess what the number one time waster is? Television! And with the explosive growth of cable, this device can consume unbelievable amounts of our time. Another big time waster is idle conversation.

As you develop the habit of planning the use of your time, you will see a reduction in unprofitable time spent. Continue the process of planning and work to improve one day at a time. Focus on the next twenty-four hours and remember the old saying, "DO NOT squander time; it is the stuff life is made of."

ACTION STEP:

Start to use a system that will allow you to keep a record of the use of your time each day for the next three months. At the end of each week, take a red pen and circle the areas that you would label "time wasters" and mark (TW). At the same time, work to plan the next day or coming week. Start with simple things and work up to more involved details.

FOR FURTHER READING:

The Time Trap: The New Version of the Classic Book on Time Management
chapters 1 and 2, pp. 3–26
Alec Mackenzie

Section 7

A DISCIPLINED LIFE

41
Reading

Also bring my books, and especially my papers (2 Timothy 4:13).

This was one of the final requests of a condemned man. He knew he had very little time to live, yet one of the most important things in this life to him were papers to read. The apostle Paul knew the value of reading. He recognized that reading was a primary gateway to knowledge. We can see the value he placed on this activity. He understood that reading was one of the wonderful gifts God had bestowed on mankind.

Through the ages, reading has played a critical role in the development of our understanding. God has chosen the written word as the vehicle to share and instruct us on who He is and how we are to live.

Reading is not only essential to all areas of learning, but it can be extremely enjoyable. As with almost any activity, though, it requires practice to learn to do it well. There are different types of reading and different ways to read. The two most important points to remember about reading are: (1) to develop the habit of reading, and (2) to strengthen your ability to read and comprehend.

As with most disciplines, the more you practice reading, the better you become; and the better you become, the more enjoyment you realize. The real secret to becoming good at reading is to begin with things that interest you and to do it daily.

Reading serves another critical role that can impact our entire lives—namely, it serves to keep our minds sharp, active, and growing. Unfortunately, many people were never trained well in reading nor encouraged to pursue it. Consequently, those people don't like to read. If this is your situation I recommend that you seek out new products at a bookstore that are designed to help people improve their reading skills. Do whatever it takes to learn or improve this wonderful activity.

I close with a quote from Oswald Chambers, author of *My Utmost For His Highest*: "That is the way God speaks to us; not by visions and dreams, but by words. When a man gets to God, it is by the most simple way —words."

ACTION STEP:

Pick out one book related to the Christian life you have been interested in reading but have not found the time to do so. Get a copy and set a goal to read some every day. Work to stay consistent.

FOR FURTHER READING:

The Books You Read
pages 5–30
Edited by Charles E. Jones

42

Journaling

···❀···

For the weapons of our warfare are not carnal but mighty in God for pulling down strongholds, casting down arguments and every high thing that exalts itself against the knowledge of God, bringing every thought into captivity to the obedience of Christ (2 Corinthians 10:4–5 NKJV).

One of the most important truths our Lord made clear in His teachings to the disciples was that a life pleasing to God starts from the inside and moves outward. The real key to victorious Christian living is the keeping of the heart and the mind. Who we are on the inside—our thought life—ultimately displays who we are to the rest of the world.

One of the spiritual disciplines that can be especially constructive in helping us see a picture of our thought life is journaling. This is the activity of writing a daily record of occurrences or observations. It can be very simple or quite extensive. With this process, we can begin to better understand who we are and the feelings and meditations that occupy our minds. It is an excellent exercise to assist us in dealing with our emotions and in setting them in the proper perspective. It can serve to pinpoint areas where specific prayer is needed. It is also a wonderful tool to capture the times that our thoughts are directed toward God and the issues of His kingdom. Journaling can be one of the best introductions to a dedicated time of daily devotions that you can practice.

·····

Journaling can also be an effective medium in making decisions. As various issues confront us each day, the process of recording thoughts, impressions, and leadings from the Holy Spirit can be reviewed at a critical point before you reach a decision. Another valuable benefit of journaling is the guidance and leading you can gain by your daily records. The directives of the Holy Spirit are usually gently repeated and reinforced messages that come to us in many different ways and that always line up with scriptural truth. With journaling it is possible to see these messages clearly develop over time in your written notes. Journaling also provides a wonderful vehicle to clarify your beliefs and commitments in writing. When you express something in writing, it usually becomes much more a part of who you are and how you think.

Lastly, journaling is very helpful in opening up the creative ideas and thoughts that form in your mind. You will be amazed at the value and impact of these mental images that otherwise would be lost. There is no one correct way to journal. It is very personal and should be geared to who you are. Some will write pages and pages, others only a few sentences. Both are valuable. The main thing is to try it and discover the wonderful potential journaling will give to you in your life as a believer.

ACTION STEP:

Decide on a simple way for you to journal something every day for one month. Write down your thoughts, feelings, and what you believe the Holy Spirit is saying to you. Evaluate your writing and see if it has benefited you.

_____

FOR FURTHER READING:

How to Keep a Spiritual Journal
chapters 1 and 2, pp. 9–30
Ronald Klug

43
Organizing

Good planning and hard work lead to prosperity, but hasty shortcuts lead to poverty (Proverbs 21:5).

One of the most familiar "cries for help" today comes from people who are not able to cope with the avalanche of information, activities, and other things that daily enter their lives. Too much to do is now commonplace. One way to help control this is to get organized. Getting organized is learning to develop ways to handle all the details that inundate us each day. For the believer, organization is critical in assisting us to keep Jesus Christ at the center of our lives. It is so easy in this day and time to become so busy that we lose sight of what is most important.

A large majority of people never design and undertake a program to help themselves become better organized. For the most part, people just get by when it comes to managing the hectic pace of life's ever-increasing demands. Here are some basics that can make a big difference in one's productivity and accomplishments.

As usual, the place to start is to assess your answer to the question: How organized are you? I suggest you break down your life into a number of different categories to aid you in making this evaluation. Start with your spiritual life. Do you keep things in a way that encourages and assists you in doing the daily activities that are essential to healthy spiritual well-being? Next, go to your home life. Are your important records, files, and bills organized? Are the things you read accessible? How are your drawers, desk, and closets? How often do you waste time looking for a lost item? Review your situation at work. Ask the same types of questions.

When you have completed this examination, you will probably discover that you are like most people: You require assistance. If this is true, the second step is to ask yourself, *How organized do I need to be, and how organized would I like to be?* Begin with the essentials, then progress to how you would like to be organized in other areas of your life.

One absolutely essential step that must be made if you are to get organized is to set a plan of action and a system to implement that plan. As you did with your initial evaluation, divide your life into sections: work, business, home, family, spiritual, and others. An excellent model to review is the *Believer's Life System,* discussed in appendix A of this book. After you have determined your sections, decide the important things that should be done regularly. Organize around these priorities. Work at a system that fits you. Make it flexible and easy to use. Start with basics such as a daily calendar with key appointments or key dates and work from there. Add new categories if needed. Eliminate things that don't seem beneficial. Over time you will be amazed at the positive results you will gain.

ACTION STEP:

Be sure to read the appendices, especially appendix A, in this book. Make a note of the things that you think might benefit you as you start to get organized. Develop a simple step-by-step plan to becoming more organized.

FOR FURTHER READING:

Organize Yourself!
part one, pp. 5–29
Ronni Eisenberg

44
Budgeting

⁓

And the Lord replied, "I'm talking to any faithful, sensible servant to whom the master gives the responsibility of managing his household and feeding his family. If the master returns and finds that the servant has done a good job, there will be a reward. I assure you, the master will put that servant in charge of all he owns" (Luke 12:42–44).

If someone were to ask you the major reason for the high rate of divorce in this country, you would probably be amazed to learn that the answer is associated with money. Yes, money! Clearly, this is why the Bible has so much to say about the subject. The use or abuse of money is a dominant theme in most people's lives, and, therefore, it is essential to know how to understand, manage, and protect this item that God has allowed to be a part of each life. The art of the administration of your money is called budgeting. This is a foundational discipline in becoming a good steward of the money the Lord has given you.

The primary starting point for believers is to examine how they think about money. Some people pay no attention to the subject and consequently make poor decisions in how they use money. Others love money and are driven by this preoccupation—to their detriment. Many pay little attention but tend to consistently spend more than they earn and end up borrowing against future earnings. The reality is that if we don't handle money as good stewards, we will become enslaved to it and face the consequences of that enslavement.

The next step is to make sure you have truly turned every part of your life, including your pocketbook, over to the Lord. From there you need to establish a goal to develop a budget that you will use as a tool to help you manage your money. Determine to stop bad habits such as buying on credit. Plan to pay down credit cards or other short-term debt. Watch for places where you practice wasteful spending. After you have addressed the short-term goals, take a look at some of the long-term goals in the budgeting area. Maybe you don't own your own home. Initiate a plan to someday achieve this goal. Without budgeting, achievement of your goals will never occur.

Some believers may already be living on a budget and do a good job with the basics of managing their money. This may be a good time to work on establishing a budget to improve the use of your time. Many feel that in today's society their time is the most valuable asset they have. There are many who manage their money, but don't manage time very well. Here, too, a budget approach can be very beneficial.

The starting point in learning how to take care of God's money and time is to start using the discipline of a budget. Ask any businessperson if he or she knows of a business that successfully operates without the budget process. The answer will be "no." The same is true in your personal life.

ACTION STEP:

Make a commitment to record in writing every expenditure you and your family have over a one-month period. Compare that with your income. This is a good place to start putting together a budget. Make certain your budget starts with giving to God.

FOR FURTHER READING:

How to Manage Your Money
sections 5 and 6, pp. 45–62
Larry Burkett

45
Diet and Exercise

* ⟡ *

Physical exercise has some value, but spiritual exercise is much more important, for it promises a reward in both this life and the next (1 Timothy 4:8).

One clear indication that most Christians don't read their Bibles regularly and don't apply biblical truths to their lives is today's unbelievable obsession with fad diets and the preoccupation with exercise and physical fitness in the church. It is not that we should neglect our bodily health; we should be mindful of it. But when held in balance, it is a minor thing compared with the need of keeping ourselves spiritually fit. It is with this truth in mind that we should think about diet and exercise.

The Bible says that our bodies are the temple of the living God. Therefore we should be concerned with both our spiritual and physical needs. It is obvious that most people eat too much food, and usually the wrong kinds. In many cases, a diet is necessary to try to correct the consequences of choices of the food you eat or of overeating in general. Exercise on a routine basis is another area we tend to exclude.

Proper eating habits and exercise are important for good physical health, especially for believers. Overeating, poor decisions in what we eat, and lack of exercise are all poor choices that have developed into bad habits. In order to change this situation it is important to recognize the problem and make a decided effort to work on building good practices based on good choices.

Here are some simple guidelines to think about and begin to apply to your specific situation. First, start all things with prayer. Ask God to help you establish good habits to replace bad ones. Second, determine to initiate one good habit with your diet. Begin with something small, but work hard to practice it daily. Third, develop a routine of exercise. Maybe it will be to take a short walk every day. The critical concern is to build it into your daily schedule. Fourth, think about a reasonable goal that you would like to reach and a reasonable time needed to reach it.

The most important key is to start! Start small and build as you go. Make sure you perform your goals daily. Over a process of time, it will become a natural part of your everyday life. Don't expect quick fixes. This is unrealistic and is the focus of hyperpromotion ads and fairy tales. With God's help, you will be able to realize successful results toward your intended goals in the areas of good nutrition and exercise.

ACTION STEP:

Make a list of bad habits you have developed over the past few years in both your diet and exercise. Choose one item from each area and make a specific goal to change it to a good habit. After three months, evaluate your progress and repeat the process.

FOR FURTHER READING:

It's Better to Believe
chapters 1 and 2, pp. 3–20
Kenneth H. Cooper, M.D.

46

Studying

And the people of Berea were more open-minded than those in Thessalonica, and they listened eagerly to Paul's message. They searched the Scriptures day after day to check up on Paul and Silas, to see if they were really teaching the truth (Acts 17:11).

We have all heard the expression "It's never too late to learn." The older I get, the more I appreciate the truth of that statement. The capacity of the human mind is a phenomenon beyond anything we can conceive, and it still holds mysteries that modern science has not yet uncovered. God has provided us with an unbelievable potential for learning. Unfortunately, much of that energy is never used. One of the major reasons people don't learn more is that they have never mastered the discipline of how to study. Getting a grip on how to study is the gateway to learning and all of its rewards.

If you want to learn how to study better, start by taking an assessment of your current study habits or analyze to what degree your study habits were developed when you were in school. Some people never cultivated good study skills. Therefore, they have lost much of the desire to learn new things. Others who may have at one time engaged their minds in good practices have since let them lie dormant so that the exercise has become rusty and unused. You can also do a simple inventory of what you think your problem areas are. Compare these with some of the points I am going to discuss.

Learning how to study is a process that takes time and practice. After you have determined what level of ability you are at, set some simple goals to help you improve. Make sure you create good supports for your efforts. Determine the place where you seem to study best and think about the things you have the greatest interest in learning.

Without question, your reading and comprehension skills will have the greatest impact on your ability to study. As believers, good reading skills are absolutely necessary if we are going to be people of the Book. Depending on your level of proficiency, the best advice I can give you is to start building from that place. Get a simple book on the "how to" of reading.

After reading and comprehension, the next most important component of studying is making the best use of your time. There is little argument that most people waste a lot of time, and that is why those who have mastered the management of their time have also developed good study habits. Go back and reread my discussion on "Planning" and "Time Management." Both of these topics will help you see how to better optimize your time.

The third critical area of studying is how to take good notes—from lectures, Sunday school classes, sermons, books, and so on. The key to learning to take good notes is to keep it short. Invent your own short-hand and practice using it. Over time you will see how well it works. Make a habit to review it later to see if you understand what you noted. Use whatever devices work to capture what you want to learn. Symbols and graphics also help. Trial and error is the bottom line in learning good note taking.

Remember, as you master the art of studying, you are mastering part of the art of learning, and that should be a lifelong activity. A willingness to learn is a characteristic of a truly wise person.

ACTION STEP:

Make a commitment to improve your discipline of study. Write down some ways you will accomplish this goal. Begin to apply these steps in your regular routine of study.

FOR FURTHER READING:

How to Study
Ron Fry

Section 8

A GOAL-ORIENTED LIFE

47

Balance

⚬

In all your ways acknowledge Him, and He will make your paths straight (Proverbs 3:6 NASB).

Genuine and wholesome spirituality is the goal of all Christian living." This quote by Dr. Charles Ryrie is the central theme of his classic book *Balancing the Christian Life*. Dr. Ryrie defines genuine as that which is biblical, and he defines wholesome as that which is balanced. Although simple, this statement represents two major challenges that play a dominant role in our lives as believers.

Developing a biblical worldview, where everything is tested against the Word of God, necessitates study of the Bible, prayer, and the guidance of the Holy Spirit. It requires time to grow and manifest itself in mature believers. It is a never-ending process that begins with the new birth and continues until we join the Lord in heaven.

Likewise, balance in every area of our lives is something we never completely achieve, although significant progress in that area is both possible and desirable. Balance in the believer's life is critical to help us guard against excesses that can be destructive and harmful to ourselves and to others. The forces of Satan have been very successful over the centuries in the lives of numerous believers who, with the best of motives, have gone to excesses that ultimately brought shame, ridicule, and divisiveness to the church. This is why becoming grounded in the Word of God is the only protection from this possibility.

Growing in the understanding of our own personality is another area that can help in avoiding tendencies to get out of balance. God has created in each of us different types of personalities. Some believers are more prone to criticism than others; some are more emotional; others are less discerning. Each person possesses individuality. As we understand ourselves better, we should learn to protect against the areas where we are apt to get out of balance.

Learning about the life of Christ and striving to be conformed to His image serves as our prime example in accomplishing balance. Balance ultimately comes from a deepening relationship with Jesus Christ as we learn of His perfect ways in every area of life. This, too, is a lifelong progression.

ACTION STEP:

Take the time to sit down and reflect on your daily activities over the past week. Ask yourself if there are some areas that you would label "out of balance." Make a point to work on these areas.

FOR FURTHER READING:

Balancing the Christian Life
Charles C. Ryrie

48

Moderation

··⚬··

People who work hard sleep well, whether they eat little or much. But the rich are always worrying and seldom get a good night's sleep (Ecclesiastes 5:12).

One of the most interesting new businesses that has developed over the past ten years is the business of mini-storage companies. I am sure you have seen them, since they seem to be everywhere, even in the most unexpected places. I have been amazed at the growth, expansion, and proliferation of this industry. It is clear that this is a thriving business. No doubt there are many good reasons that this is true, but I suspect it is an indication of America's obsession with "more." If you wonder whether this is overstating a point, take a look at the thriving increase of television channels made available by way of satellite.

Have you noticed the new types of movie theaters being built today—twenty, thirty, or more theaters in one complex? Everywhere you turn in our culture today, we are confronted with the phenomenon of "more." *Excessive,* I believe, has certainly become the watchword of the nineties. One of the real questions of life in our times, even for believers, is "How much is enough?" When do we pass from being blessed from God to becoming like the world around us and its preoccupation with "stuff"?

Here again, we can go to the Bible to find some concrete answers. There are numerous examples of affluent and prosperous believers in the Bible. It is evident that God chooses to grant extra measures of prosperity to some . But it is equally apparent that God's blessings are meant to be a used as a means to provide funding for His kingdom. Lavish lifestyles are not a good testimony and do not demonstrate good stewardship in the lives of Christians. As we study the Word of God, we should become convinced that moderation should be a key word in all areas of our lives. This is especially true when it comes to establishing a lifestyle and standard of living. Believers, more than anyone else, need to examine the amount of stress caused by the demands of "things" that encumber their lives. It takes time and energy to shop for, buy, and maintain "things." Every human being has a limited amount of time, energy, and funds. If these are overly used for self, giving to God goes lacking. This, sadly, is what is taking place in a large percentage of Christians' lives today. Many of us spend so much of our time, money, and energy in other areas of life that God, who has given us all things, is given back very little.

If this trend is to be altered, it must begin with each individual believer resolving to apply the discipline of moderation in his life. Each of us needs to establish how much is enough and then pray for wisdom to live by that standard.

ACTION STEP:

Make an assessment of where you are in today's culture regarding your lifestyle. If there are areas you would determine to be in the "excessive" category, make plans to alter them.

FOR FURTHER READING:

The ABC's of Wisdom
pages 13–43
Ray Pritchard

49

Simplicity

·····················&·····························

But seek first the kingdom of God and His righteousness, and all these things shall be added to you (Matthew 6:33 NKJV).

As we approach the beginning of the twenty-first century, there is one subject on which most people would agree, and that is the complexity of life. Over the past fifty years we have seen an unbelievable transition in lifestyle, the pace with which we live, and the demands that consume our time. We have shifted from an industrial-based economy to an information-based economy. Instead of a sizable population living in rural areas, we now have an influx of people in the suburbs and cities. Most families now contain two wage earners instead of only one.

Opportunities open to families today are mind-boggling. Every member of the family has more and more occasions to be involved with sports, projects, and all types of group activities. The availabilities for educational activities have mushroomed. Now there are countless ways you can earn a degree or an advanced degree or just work on a subject of interest. In the area of our careers there are great opportunities in new industries spawned by the advent of many new technologies. With greater earnings many are now able to participate in the investment market. Leisure affords us so many options that it is impossible even to keep up with all the choices. Alternatives in the arena of spectator sports are overwhelming. There is now so much to do, to see, to watch. It is no wonder the process of selection has become complex in itself.

We believers must beware of the danger of all these things drawing us away from what should always be our first priority. Many have been too consumed in all that is available today and have left their first love, Jesus Christ. Many have not matured as they should and are still babes in Christ. God has wonderfully provided believers with discretion on how to manage all the complexities of this life and, more importantly, how to avoid the anxiety that so often accompanies these complexities. It is a simple command with a wonderful promise. "But seek first the kingdom of God and His righteousness, and all these things shall be added to you" (Matthew 6:33 NKJV). As believers, we are to aim at and strive after His kingdom and pursue becoming more like Christ and His righteousness. When we put God first in everything, all else will actually become better. Followed daily, this simple guideline can have profound impact on every area of our lives.

ACTION STEP:

Take a 3-by-5 index card or a Post-it note and write out Matthew 6:31–34. Read it every day and think about how it can be applied to your life. Work to redirect any worries to faith in God's promises.

FOR FURTHER READING:

Celebration of Discipline
chapter 6, pp. 79–95
Richard J. Foster

50
Commitment

· ✀ ·

Love the Lord your God with all your heart and with all your soul and with all your strength (Deuteronomy 6:5 NIV).

The act of commitment is, for the most part, a lost practice in today's culture. The phrase "My word is my bond" has been replaced with a spectrum of excuses. Unfortunately, many people today do not embrace the concept of commitment, whether it is in relationship to God, to a mate or family, to work, or to just about anything associated with personal resolve.

The Bible explains that selfishness is the principle cause for lack of commitment. The tragic story is told of King David in 2 Samuel 11, which tells us how his disobedience to God led him to fail in his example as the leader of Israel, as a husband, and as the commander of his generals. Had David stayed committed to his role as Israel's leader, he would have been at the head of his army instead of remaining at his palace when "kings went forth to battle." If David had attended to his own household instead of allowing his eyes to lust, he would not have found himself entrapped in the act of adultery. And had David's duty to his general been noble, he would not have used his position to murder the husband of the woman with whom he had an adulterous relationship.

Commitment is an exercise of the will. Commitment also requires the avoidance of circumstances that pull us away from commitment. The best way to maintain all other commitments is to diligently remain faithful in our daily relationship with God. Work to understand your vulnerability and build defenses to protect against failure. Pray for strength to keep commitments. Pray to be a person of your word.

ACTION STEP:

Make a list of areas where you live up to your commitments; then make a list of areas where you fail to keep those commitments. Then list some ways to learn from the first list so that you can improve on the second list.

FOR FURTHER READING:

The Power of Commitment
Jerry White

51

Perseverance

······································· ✄ ·······························

Therefore, my beloved brethren, be steadfast, immovable, always abounding in the work of the Lord, knowing that in the Lord your labor is not in vain (1 Corinthians 15:58 RSV).

In my office at home I have a picture and a bust of one of my favorite heroes, Abraham Lincoln. There is almost no question in my mind that he was our greatest president. He played a major role in holding our nation together at its most troubled time. As a believer, he recognized the need for dependence on God and was clearly a man of prayer. Abraham Lincoln was a friendly man, given to storytelling and humor, and he was a person of great passion and pity for his fellowman.

Of all Lincoln's qualities—and they are numerous—the one that stands out most to me is his perseverance. You are probably familiar with the long list of ventures he pursued but failed. Among these, he started two businesses that failed and lost numerous runs for office. His perseverance and his steadfastness were amazing.

The Bible speaks a lot about perseverance. It teaches that perseverance leads to character. One of the great character studies of the Bible is that of Joseph. As you read and study his life, you are struck with his persistence in the face of hopelessness. He neither gave up nor lost hope. As the Bible tells us, "The Lord was with Joseph and blessed him greatly" (Genesis 39:2). Joseph grew in character.

Maybe one reason for lack of character development in this day is the loss of the quality of perseverance. It does not take much attention to recognize that this is a lost attribute from many areas of our society. Instant gratification is the focus and the characteristic that wars against perseverance.

How do we develop this principle in ourselves or strengthen it to become an integral part of our personalities? As believers, we have all been given the gift of the Holy Spirit, but many times we fail to walk in the Spirit. One of the best ways to strengthen our perseverance is to pray and ask the Holy Spirit for help in developing this trait in our lives. We can expect obstacles, disappointments, and failures to come into our lives. The key is to be alert to the opportunities that are part of every experience of life. God the Holy Spirit's desire is that we learn to persist and endure, and He is eager to help us in the process.

Another important element is learning to pray for others. It will transform your attitude, especially in terms of self-centeredness and impatience. You will have your eyes opened to the struggles of others and of many examples of perseverance in others. Another way to learn perseverance is to communicate with close friends and be open and honest with them. Perspectives from friends help all of us to see things in better balance. Finally, just become more aware of the need to develop this virtue in yourself.

ACTION STEP:

*Make a list of areas where you think you demonstrate
perseverance. Then, make a list of areas where you
believe you need to improve. Look up the words* perseverance *and* steadfastness *in your Bible concordance and note the verses and people related in each
instance.*

FOR FURTHER READING:

Lincoln
David Herbert Donald

52
Contentment

Let your conduct be without covetousness; be content with such things as you have. For He Himself has said, "I will never leave you nor forsake you" (Hebrews 13:5 NKJV).

One of the heart's deepest desires, but one which eludes most everyone, is contentment. Take a moment to think about the ads you have seen over the past few days. With rare exception, most will in some way appeal to the yearning for contentment. From A to Z, products are promoted in such a way as to suggest that they will provide some degree of contentment. Yet, as we all can attest, things never bring real gratification to our lives.

Another approach used to capture contentment is through relationships with others. Relationships are important—some are vital—but even these will not provide complete fulfillment. Sports, hobbies, careers, and other types of activities are also used as substitutes by many to satisfy the hunger for contentment. In the final analysis, none of these will fill that basic need. The Bible, in the book of Ecclesiastes, declares that all the things in this world will not bring lasting satisfaction.

Is there such a thing as "true contentment" and can it be attained in this life? From the book of Philippians, the apostle Paul give us some insights on the subject:

But I rejoiced in the Lord greatly that now at last your care for me has flourished again; though you surely did care, but you lacked opportunity. Not that I speak in regard to need, for I have learned in whatever state I am, to be content: I know how to be abased, and I know how to abound. Everywhere and in all things I have learned both to be full and to be hungry, both to abound and to suffer need. I can do all things through Christ who strengthens me. (Philippians 4:10–13 NKJV)

The secret to contentment, as with all things, lies in our relationship with God. It is not based on circumstances but depends on the Lord, who orders those circumstances. As our relationship with Christ deepens, we will grow in grace and contentment in all things. As we strive to shift the focus from self to others, our contentment will grow. Dwelling more on the love of God, the mercy of God, and the grace of God will increase our contentment.

ACTION STEP:

Make a list of the blessings God has given to you. Reflect on how the world distracts us from the contentment that we should draw from these blessings. Start each day with thanksgiving to God.

FOR FURTHER READING:

Far from Home: The Soul's Search for Intimacy with God introduction and chapters 1 and 2, pp. 11–42
Joseph M. Stowell

Summary

One of the intrinsic truths about mankind is that we have been patterned after and created in the image of God. God has chosen to fashion us in a way that reflects some of His wonderful characteristics, and He has provided a way for man to enjoy personal fellowship with Himself. We see a picture of that fellowship in the book of Genesis when Adam and Eve enjoyed a direct relationship with the Triune God. Tragically, sin entered the arena and the result was separation from God. By God's grace, He has enabled us to have that relationship reestablished through His Son.

At the moment of our regeneration (our new birth), we are introduced to God by the work of the Holy Spirit. We come to Him and He accepts us just as we are. From that point, God begins to rebuild our lives and our relationship with Him. That process of rebuilding is called sanctification. It is one of the main works of the Holy Spirit in our lives. It is a slow process that takes a lifetime. It is possible for each one of us to respond and cooperate with the Holy Spirit in our sanctification, just as it is possible to miss out on opportunities given to us by God to grow and become more like the Lord.

The gateway God has dispensed to each of us in this rebuilding process is our mind. It is through the renewing of our minds by the Word of God and by the power of His Holy Spirit that God produces a growing, healthy believer who, as he matures, is transformed into the person God desires him to be—into the image of His Son. Each day, if we submit to God's work in our lives, our growth will manifest itself in various ways. Our relationship with God will deepen. We will become more of the salt and light in this world, which He intended us to be. We will lovingly apply and live out His commandments. The love of God will manifest itself in our lives to others. And each day, with God's help and if we are growing, our fellowship with our Lord will grow sweeter and sweeter, as it was meant to be.

In closing, I want to leave you with this quotation from the Bible. It is from my favorite book, Paul's letter to the Romans. It is the very best summary I could leave with you:

> And so, dear brothers and sisters, I plead with you to give your bodies to God. Let them be a living and holy sacrifice—the kind he will accept. When you think of what he has done for you, is this too much to ask? Don't copy the behavior and customs of this world, but let God transform you into a new person by changing the way you think. Then you will know what God wants you to do, and you will know how good and pleasing and perfect his will really is. (Romans 12:1–2)

May God bless you and keep you and guide you on your journey.

. . . . .

Appendix A
Tools for the Journey

· ❧ ·

As I wrote in an earlier chapter of this book, I grew up around the construction business. One of those "little things" I learned that make a real difference over the long run is the importance of having the right tools when you get ready to do a specific job. A number of things result when this principle of wisdom is applied. On an overall basis, you will produce a better product and usually the activity will be accomplished in less time. Another result is that less effort is required and, in many cases, what could have been a real chore turns into a very enjoyable task. Having the right type of tool makes a real difference in any undertaking. The same can be said in the journey of every believer —the right tools are essential to fruitful living.

At the risk of being too elementary, I suggest that the first basic need of each believer is a good study Bible. This type of Bible provides explanatory notes and a great deal of valuable reference materials such as tables, charts, and lists. Today there are numerous excellent study Bibles on the market. Here are just a few that I recommend: *The Expanded Ryrie Study Bible, The John MacArthur Study Bible, The NIV Study Bible,* and *The Life Application Study Bible.*

Regarding translations, there are two major types, both of which are excellent for general use. The first is called "formal equivalence," and its objective is to attempt a word-to-word translation. The New American Standard translation is one of the most popular "formal equivalence" translations. The second is called "dynamic equivalence," and its objective is to produce a thought-for-thought translation. The New International Version and The New Living Translation are outstanding examples of this kind. Both types of translations provide strong points and both are valuable for Bible study. It is important to remember that the Bible we have today in any number of translations is totally trustworthy and accurate. It is God's library for man, made up of sixty-six books written over a time span of fifteen hundred years.

The second tool that every believer should own is a good exhaustive concordance of the Bible. Some of the best are *The New Strong's Exhaustive Concordance of the Bible* published by Nelson (KJV), *NIV Exhaustive Concordance* published by Zondervan, and *NAS Exhaustive Concordance of the Bible* published by Foundation Publications. This tool allows the Bible to interpret itself and enables the user to locate every place that a specific word is used in Scripture as well as every Hebrew or Greek word related to it. A concordance will help you as you begin to apply the inductive method of studying the Bible. (See chapter 17 on Bible Study. Remember: Observation, Interpretation, Application.)

Another important aid that can become invaluable in your growth as a believer is a group of products called *The Believer's Life System.* It is based on the loose-leaf organizer concept but is much, much more than just an organizer. *The Believer's Life System* is an extremely flexible and adaptable system of products designed to help a believer consolidate a number of features in a binder that you can keep with you all the time. These products can assist and encourage you and help you structure your time in such things as Bible reading, Bible study, prayer, devotions, Bible memory, and many other spiritual disciplines. It contains planning calendars and dated pages as well as pages for daily, weekly, and monthly scheduling. It provides many more items such as recommended reading lists, key Scripture verses, and profound quotes. It is truly a complete "toolbox" for believers.

The last bit of counsel I wish to convey is to encourage every believer to read and use good books to complement their study of the Bible. God has blessed us with an exceptional number of valuable titles that can enrich our learning. Discover how books can become some of your best friends—the more you read them, the better they get. Locate your local Christian bookstore or call 1-800-991-7747 to find out the location of the nearest Christian bookstore, and start your own library!

How to Use This Book

As has been mentioned several times, the main goal of this book is to encourage and help believers grow in their knowledge and service for God through learning and applying various disciplines that will affect their daily lives. One excellent way that can be accomplished is to commit to the following program.

1. Pray and ask God to help you in your commitment to this program.
2. Select both a date and a time that you are going to form a habit of doing this discipline. I would strongly recommend a Sunday afternoon or evening.
3. Select a good place that is comfortable and quiet and conducive to your concentration.
4. Be sure you have a good study Bible, an exhaustive concordance, paper or a journal, pen, pencil, and eraser.
5. Start by reading one topic per week from this book.
6. Read the pages that are suggested in "For Further Reading."
7. Lay out a schedule to practice and complete the Action Step over the coming week.

8. Work hard to become consistent and faithful to your goals.
9. Chart your progress and record what you do each week.
10. Stick with it!

In most cases, this will not take more than thirty to forty minutes each week. After doing this exercise for a few weeks, you should be able to sense a habit taking shape. Most important, you will begin to experience the pleasure of growing in your faith.

Appendix C
Bible Reading Plan

JANUARY

	MORNING	EVENING		MORNING	EVENING
1.	GEN. 1, 2	MATT. 1	17.	GEN. 41	MATT. 13:1–32
2.	GEN. 3, 4, 5	MATT. 2	18.	GEN. 42, 43	MATT. 13:33–58
3.	GEN. 6, 7, 8	MATT. 3	19.	GEN. 44, 45	MATT. 14:1–21
4.	GEN. 9, 10, 11	MATT. 4	20.	GEN. 46, 47, 48	MATT. 14:22–36
5.	GEN. 12, 13, 14	MATT. 5:1–26	21.	GEN. 49, 50	MATT. 15:1–20
6.	GEN. 15, 16, 17	MATT. 5:27–48	22.	EX. 1, 2, 3	MATT. 15:21–39
7.	GEN. 18, 19	MATT. 6	23.	EX. 4, 5, 6	MATT. 16
8.	GEN. 20, 21, 22	MATT. 7	24.	EX. 7, 8	MATT. 17
9.	GEN. 23, 24	MATT. 8	25.	EX. 9, 10	MATT. 18:1–20
10.	GEN. 25, 26	MATT. 9:1–17	26.	EX. 11, 12	MATT. 18:21–35
11.	GEN. 27, 28	MATT. 9:18–38	27.	EX. 13, 14, 15	MATT. 19:1–15
12.	GEN. 29, 30	MATT. 10:1–23	28.	EX. 16, 17, 18	MATT. 19:16–30
13.	GEN. 31, 32	MATT. 10:24–42	29.	EX. 19, 20, 21	MATT. 20:1–16
14.	GEN. 33, 34, 35	MATT. 11	30.	EX. 22, 23, 24	MATT. 20:17–34
15.	GEN. 36, 37	MATT. 12:1–21	31.	EX. 25, 26	MATT. 21:1–22
16.	GEN. 38, 39, 40	MATT. 12:22–50			

FEBRUARY

	MORNING	EVENING		MORNING	EVENING
1.	EX. 27, 28	MATT. 21:23–46	16.	LEV. 22, 23	MARK 1:1–22
2.	EX. 29, 30	MATT. 22:1–22	17.	LEV. 24, 25	MARK 1:23–45
3.	EX. 31, 32, 33	MATT. 22:23–46	18.	LEV. 26, 27	MARK 2
4.	EX. 34, 35, 36	MATT. 23:1–22	19.	NUM. 1, 2	MARK 3:1–21
5.	EX. 37, 38	MATT. 23:23–39	20.	NUM. 3, 4	MARK 3:22–35
6.	EX. 39, 40	MATT. 24:1–22	21.	NUM. 5, 6	MARK 4:1–20
7.	LEV. 1, 2, 3	MATT. 24:23–51	22.	NUM. 7	MARK 4:21–41
8.	LEV. 4, 5, 6	MATT. 25:1–30	23.	NUM. 8, 9, 10	MARK 5:1–20
9.	LEV. 7, 8, 9	MATT. 25:31–46	24.	NUM. 11, 12, 13	MARK 5:21–43
10.	LEV. 10, 11, 12	MATT. 26:1–19	25.	NUM. 14, 15	MARK 6:1–32
11.	LEV. 13	MATT. 26:20–54	26.	NUM. 16, 17	MARK 6:33–56
12.	LEV. 14	MATT. 26:55–75	27.	NUM. 18, 19, 20	MARK 7:1–13
13.	LEV. 15, 16, 17	MATT. 27:1–31	28.	NUM. 21, 22	MARK 7:14–37
14.	LEV. 18, 19	MATT. 27:32–66	29.	NUM. 23, 24, 25	MARK 8:1–21
15.	LEV. 20, 21	MATT. 28:1–20			

Divide chapters for Feb. 29 and read them Feb. 28 and Mar.1 when February has only 28 days.

MARCH

MORNING	EVENING	MORNING	EVENING
1. NUM. 26, 27	MARK 8:22–38	17. DEUT. 29, 30	MARK 16
2. NUM. 28, 29	MARK 9:1–29	18. DEUT. 31, 32	LUKE 1:1–23
3. NUM. 30, 31	MARK 9:30–50	19. DEUT. 33, 34	LUKE 1:24–56
4. NUM. 32, 33	MARK 10:1–31	20. JOSH. 1, 2, 3	LUKE 1:57–80
5. NUM. 34, 35, 36	MARK 10:32–52	21. JOSH. 4, 5, 6	LUKE 2:1–24
6. DEUT. 1, 2	MARK 11:1–19	22. JOSH. 7, 8	LUKE 2:25–52
7. DEUT. 3, 4	MARK 11:20–33	23. JOSH. 9, 10	LUKE 3
8. DEUT. 5, 6, 7	MARK 12:1–27	24. JOSH. 11, 12, 13	LUKE 4:1–32
9. DEUT. 8, 9, 10	MARK 12:28–44	25. JOSH. 14, 15	LUKE 4:33–44
10. DEUT. 11, 12, 13	MARK 13:1–13	26. JOSH. 16, 17, 18	LUKE 5:1–16
11. DEUT. 14, 15, 16	MARK 13:14–37	27. JOSH. 19, 20	LUKE 5:17–39
12. DEUT. 17, 18, 19	MARK 14:1–25	28. JOSH. 21, 22	LUKE 6:1–26
13. DEUT. 20, 21, 22	MARK 14:26–50	29. JOSH. 23, 24	LUKE 6:27–49
14. DEUT. 23, 24, 25	MARK 14:51–72	30. JUDG. 1, 2	LUKE 7:1–30
15. DEUT. 26, 27	MARK 15:1–26	31. JUDG. 3, 4, 5	LUKE 7:31–50
16. DEUT. 28			

APRIL

MORNING	EVENING	MORNING	EVENING
1. JUDG. 6, 7	LUKE 8:1–21	16. 1 SAM. 19, 20, 21	LUKE 15:11–32
2. JUDG. 8, 9	LUKE 8:22–56	17. 1 SAM. 22, 23, 24	LUKE 16:1–18
3. JUDG. 10, 11	LUKE 9:1–36	18. 1 SAM. 25, 26	LUKE 16:19–31
4. JUDG. 12, 13, 14	LUKE 9:37–62	19. 1 SAM. 27, 28, 29	LUKE 17:1–19
5. JUDG. 15, 16, 17	LUKE 10:1–24	20. 1 SAM. 30, 31	LUKE 17:20–37
6. JUDG. 18, 19	LUKE 10:25–42	21. 2 SAM. 1, 2, 3	LUKE 18:1–17
7. JUDG. 20, 21	LUKE 11:1–28	22. 2 SAM. 4, 5, 6	LUKE 18:18–43
8. RUTH 1, 2, 3, 4	LUKE 11:29–54	23. 2 SAM. 7, 8, 9	LUKE 19: 1–28
9. 1 SAM. 1, 2, 3	LUKE 12:1–34	24. 2 SAM. 10, 11, 12	LUKE 19:29–48
10. 1 SAM. 4, 5, 6	LUKE 12:35–59	25. 2 SAM. 13, 14	LUKE 20:1–26
11. 1 SAM. 7, 8, 9	LUKE 13:1–21	26. 2 SAM. 15, 16	LUKE 20:27–47
12. 1 SAM. 10, 11, 12	LUKE 13:22–35	27. 2 SAM. 17, 18	LUKE 21:1–19
13. 1 SAM. 13, 14	LUKE 14:1–24	28. 2 SAM. 19, 20	LUKE 21:20–38
14. 1 SAM. 15, 16	LUKE 14:25–35	29. 2 SAM. 21, 22	LUKE 22:1–30
15. 1 SAM. 17, 18	LUKE 15:1–10	30. 2 SAM. 23, 24	LUKE 22:31–53

MAY

MORNING	EVENING	MORNING	EVENING
1. 1 KINGS 1, 2	LUKE 22:54–71	17. 2 KINGS 18, 19	JOHN 6:22–44
2. 1 KINGS 3, 4, 5	LUKE 23:1–26	18. 2 KINGS 20, 21, 22	JOHN 6:45–71
3. 1 KINGS 6, 7	LUKE 23:27–38	19. 2 KINGS 23, 24, 25	JOHN 7:1–31
4. 1 KINGS 8, 9	LUKE 23:39–56	20. 1 CHR. 1, 2	JOHN 7:32–53
5. 1 KINGS 10, 11	LUKE 24:1–35	21. 1 CHR. 3, 4, 5	JOHN 8:1–20
6. 1 KINGS 12, 13	LUKE 24:36–53	22. 1 CHR. 6, 7	JOHN 8:21–36
7. 1 KINGS 14, 15	JOHN 1:1–28	23. 1 CHR. 8, 9, 10	JOHN 8:37–59
8. 1 KINGS 16, 17, 18	JOHN 1:29–51	24. 1 CHR. 11, 12, 13	JOHN 9:1–23
9. 1 KINGS 19, 20	JOHN 2	25. 1 CHR. 14, 15, 16	JOHN 9:24–41
10. 1 KINGS 21, 22	JOHN 3:1–21	26. 1 CHR. 17, 18, 19	JOHN 10:1–21
11. 2 KINGS 1, 2, 3	JOHN 3:22–36	27. 1 CHR. 20, 21, 22	JOHN 10:22–42
12. 2 KINGS 4, 5	JOHN 4:1–30	28. 1 CHR. 23, 24, 25	JOHN 11:1–17
13. 2 KINGS 6, 7, 8	JOHN 4:31–54	29. 1 CHR. 26, 27	JOHN 11:18–46
14. 2 KINGS 9, 10, 11	JOHN 5:1–24	30. 1 CHR. 28, 29	JOHN 11:47–57
15. 2 KINGS 12, 13, 14	JOHN 5:25–47	31. 2 CHR. 1, 2, 3	JOHN 12:1–19
16. 2 KINGS 15, 16, 17	JOHN 6:1–21		

JUNE

MORNING	EVENING	MORNING	EVENING
1. 2 CHR. 4, 5, 6	JOHN 12:20–50	16. NEH. 1, 2, 3	ACTS 2:1–13
2. 2 CHR. 7, 8, 9	JOHN 13:1–17	17. NEH. 4, 5, 6	ACTS 2:14–47
3. 2 CHR. 10, 11, 12	JOHN 13:18–38	18. NEH. 7, 8	ACTS 3
4. 2 CHR. 13–16	JOHN 14	19. NEH. 9, 10, 11	ACTS 4:1–22
5. 2 CHR. 17, 18, 19	JOHN 15	20. NEH. 12, 13	ACTS 4:23–37
6. 2 CHR. 20, 21, 22	JOHN 16:1–15	21. ESTHER 1, 2, 3	ACTS 5:1–16
7. 2 CHR. 23, 24, 25	JOHN 16:16–33	22. ESTHER 4, 5, 6	ACTS 5:17–42
8. 2 CHR. 26, 27, 28	JOHN 17	23. ESTHER 7–10	ACTS 6
9. 2 CHR. 29, 30, 31	JOHN 18:1–23	24. JOB 1, 2, 3	ACTS 7:1–19
10. 2 CHR. 32, 33	JOHN 18:24–40	25. JOB 4, 5, 6	ACTS 7:20–43
11. 2 CHR. 34, 35, 36	JOHN 19:1–22	26. JOB 7, 8, 9	ACTS 7:44–60
12. EZRA 1, 2	JOHN 19:23–42	27. JOB 10, 11, 12	ACTS 8:1–25
13. EZRA 3, 4, 5	JOHN 20	28. JOB 13, 14, 15	ACTS 8:26–40
14. EZRA 6, 7, 8	JOHN 21	29. JOB 16, 17, 18	ACTS 9:1–22
15. EZRA 9, 10	ACTS 1	30. JOB 19, 20	ACTS 9:23–43

JULY

Morning	Evening	Morning	Evening
1. JOB 21, 22	ACTS 10:1–23	17. PS. 22, 23, 24	ACTS 20:1–16
2. JOB 23, 24, 25	ACTS 10:24–48	18. PS. 25, 26, 27	ACTS 20:17–38
3. JOB 26, 27, 28	ACTS 11	19. PS. 28, 29, 30	ACTS 21:1–14
4. JOB 29, 30	ACTS 12	20. PS. 31, 32, 33	ACTS 21:15–40
5. JOB 31, 32	ACTS 13:1–23	21. PS. 34, 35	ACTS 22
6. JOB 33, 34	ACTS 13:24–52	22. PS. 36, 37	ACTS 23:1–11
7. JOB 35, 36, 37	ACTS 14	23. PS. 38, 39, 40	ACTS 23:12–35
8. JOB 38, 39	ACTS 15:1–21	24. PS. 41, 42, 43	ACTS 24
9. JOB 40, 41, 42	ACTS 15:22–41	25. PS. 44, 45, 46	ACTS 25
10. PS. 1, 2, 3	ACTS 16:1–15	26. PS. 47, 48, 49	ACTS 26
11. PS. 4, 5, 6	ACTS 16:16–40	27. PS. 50, 51, 52	ACTS 27:1–25
12. PS. 7, 8, 9	ACTS 17:1–15	28. PS. 53, 54, 55	ACTS 27:26–44
13. PS. 10, 11, 12	ACTS 17:16–34	29. PS. 56, 57, 58	ACTS 28:1–15
14. PS. 13–16	ACTS 18	30. PS. 59, 60, 61	ACTS 28:16–31
15. PS. 17, 18	ACTS 19:1–20	31. PS. 62, 63, 64	ROM. 1
16. PS. 19, 20, 21	ACTS 19:21–41`		

AUGUST

Morning	Evening	Morning	Evening
1. PS. 65, 66, 67	ROM. 2	17. PS. 107, 108	ROM. 15:21–33
2. PS. 68, 69	ROM. 3	18. PS. 109, 110, 111	ROM. 16
3. PS. 70, 71, 72	ROM. 4	19. PS. 112–115	1 COR. 1
4. PS. 73, 74	ROM. 5	20. PS. 116–118	1 COR. 2
5. PS. 75, 76, 77	ROM. 6	21. PS. 119:1–48	1 COR. 3
6. PS. 78	ROM. 7	22. PS. 119:49–104	1 COR. 4
7. PS. 79, 80, 81	ROM. 8:1–18	23. PS. 119:105–176	1 COR. 5
8. PS. 82, 83, 84	ROM. 8:19–39	24. PS. 120–123	1 COR. 6
9. PS. 85, 86, 87	ROM. 9	25. PS. 124–127	1 COR. 7:1–24
10. PS. 88, 89	ROM. 10	26. PS. 128–131	1 COR. 7:25–40
11. PS. 90, 91, 92	ROM. 11:1–21	27. PS. 132–135	1 COR. 8
12. PS. 93, 94, 95	ROM. 11:22–36	28. PS. 136–138	1 COR. 9
13. PS. 96, 97, 98	ROM. 12	29. PS. 139–141	1 COR. 10:1–13
14. PS. 99–102	ROM. 13	30. PS. 142–144	1 COR. 10:14–33
15. PS. 103, 104	ROM. 14	31. PS. 145–147	1 COR. 11:1–15
16. PS. 105, 106	ROM. 15:1–20		

SEPTEMBER

	MORNING	_EVENING_		_MORNING_	_EVENING_
1.	PS. 148–150	1 COR. 11:16–34	16.	PROV. 30, 31	2 COR. 8
2.	PROV. 1, 2	1 COR. 12	17.	ECCLES. 1, 2, 3	2 COR. 9
3.	PROV. 3, 4	1 COR. 13	18.	ECCLES. 4, 5, 6	2 COR. 10
4.	PROV. 5, 6	1 COR. 14:1–20	19.	ECCLES. 7, 8, 9	2 COR. 11:1–15
5.	PROV. 7, 8	1 COR. 14:21–40	20.	ECCLES. 10, 11, 12	2 COR. 11:16–33
6.	PROV. 9, 10	1 COR. 15:1–32	21.	SONGS 1, 2, 3	2 COR. 12
7.	PROV. 11, 12	1 COR. 15:33–58	22.	SONGS 4, 5	2 COR. 13
8.	PROV. 13, 14	1 COR. 16	23.	SONGS 6, 7, 8	GAL. 1
9.	PROV. 15, 16	2 COR. 1	24.	ISAIAH 1, 2, 3	GAL. 2
10.	PROV. 17, 18	2 COR. 2	25.	ISAIAH 4, 5, 6	GAL. 3
11.	PROV. 19, 20	2 COR. 3	26.	ISAIAH 7, 8, 9	GAL. 4
12.	PROV. 21, 22	2 COR. 4	27.	ISAIAH 10, 11, 12	GAL. 5
13.	PROV. 23, 24	2 COR. 5	28.	ISAIAH 13, 14, 15	GAL. 6
14.	PROV. 25, 26, 27	2 COR. 6	29.	ISAIAH 16, 17, 18	EPH. 1
15.	PROV. 28, 29	2 COR. 7	30.	ISAIAH 19, 20, 21	EPH. 2

OCTOBER

	MORNING	_EVENING_		_MORNING_	_EVENING_
1.	ISAIAH 22, 23	EPH. 3	17.	ISAIAH 62, 63, 64	1 THESS. 5
2.	ISAIAH 24, 25, 26	EPH. 4	18.	ISAIAH 65, 66	2 THESS. 1
3.	ISAIAH 27, 28	EPH. 5	19.	JER. 1, 2	2 THESS. 2
4.	ISAIAH 29, 30	EPH. 6	20.	JER. 3, 4	2 THESS. 3
5.	ISAIAH 31, 32, 33	PHIL. 1	21.	JER. 5, 6	1 TIM. 1
6.	ISAIAH 34, 35, 36	PHIL. 2	22.	JER. 7, 8	1 TIM. 2
7.	ISAIAH 37, 38	PHIL. 3	23.	JER. 9, 10	1 TIM. 3
8.	ISAIAH 39, 40	PHIL. 4	24.	JER. 11, 12, 13	1 TIM. 4
9.	ISAIAH 41, 42	COL. 1	25.	JER. 14, 15, 16	1 TIM. 5
10.	ISAIAH 43, 44	COL. 2	26.	JER. 17, 18, 19	1 TIM. 6
11.	ISAIAH 45, 46, 47	COL. 3	27.	JER. 20, 21, 22	2 TIM. 1
12.	ISAIAH 48, 49	COL. 4	28.	JER. 23, 24	2 TIM. 2
13.	ISAIAH 50, 51, 52	1 THESS. 1	29.	JER. 25, 26	2 TIM. 3
14.	ISAIAH 53, 54, 55	1 THESS. 2	30.	JER. 27, 28	2 TIM. 4
15.	ISAIAH 56, 57, 58	1 THESS. 3	31.	JER. 29, 30	TITUS 1
16.	ISAIAH 59, 60, 61				

NOVEMBER

MORNING	EVENING	MORNING	EVENING
1. JER. 31, 32	TITUS 2	16. EZEK. 13, 14, 15	HEB. 11:20–40
2. JER. 33, 34, 35	TITUS 3	17. EZEK. 16	HEB. 12
3. JER. 36, 37	PHILEMON	18. EZEK. 17, 18, 19	HEB. 13
4. JER. 38, 39	HEB. 1	19. EZEK. 20, 21	JAMES 1
5. JER. 40, 41, 42	HEB. 2	20. EZEK. 22, 23	JAMES 2
6. JER. 43, 44, 45	HEB. 3	21. EZEK. 24, 25, 26	JAMES 3
7. JER. 46, 47, 48	HEB. 4	22. EZEK. 27, 28	JAMES 4
8. JER. 49, 50	HEB. 5	23. EZEK. 29, 30, 31	JAMES 5
9. JER. 51, 52	HEB. 6	24. EZEK. 32, 33	1 PETER 1
10. LAM. 1, 2	HEB. 7	25. EZEK. 34, 35	1 PETER 2
11. LAM. 3, 4, 5	HEB. 8	26. EZEK. 36, 37	1 PETER 3
12. EZEK. 1, 2, 3	HEB. 9	27. EZEK. 38, 39	1 PETER 4
13. EZEK. 4, 5, 6	HEB. 10:1–23	28. EZEK. 40	1 PETER 5
14. EZEK. 7, 8, 9	HEB. 10:24–39	29. EZEK. 41, 42	2 PETER 1
15. EZEK. 10, 11, 12	HEB. 11:1–19	30. EZEK. 43, 44	2 PETER 2

DECEMBER

MORNING	EVENING	MORNING	EVENING
1. EZEK. 45, 46	2 PETER 3	17. OBADIAH	REV. 8
2. EZEK. 47, 48	1 JOHN 1	18. JONAH	REV. 9
3. DAN. 1, 2	1 JOHN 2	19. MICAH 1, 2, 3	REV. 10
4. DAN. 3, 4	1 JOHN 3	20. MICAH 4, 5	REV. 11
5. DAN. 5, 6	1 JOHN 4	21. MICAH 6, 7	REV. 12
6. DAN. 7, 8	1 JOHN 5	22. NAHUM	REV. 13
7. DAN. 9, 10	2 JOHN	23. HABAKKUK	REV. 14
8. DAN. 11, 12	3 JOHN	24. ZEPHANIAH	REV. 15
9. HOSEA 1–4	JUDE	25. HAGGAI	REV. 16
10. HOSEA 5–8	REV. 1	26. ZECH. 1, 2, 3	REV. 17
11. HOSEA 9, 10, 11	REV. 2	27. ZECH. 4, 5, 6	REV. 18
12. HOSEA 12, 13, 14	REV. 3	28. ZECH. 7, 8, 9	REV. 19
13. JOEL	REV. 4	29. ZECH. 10, 11, 12	REV. 20
14. AMOS 1, 2, 3	REV. 5	30. ZECH. 13, 14	REV. 21
15. AMOS 4, 5, 6	REV. 6	31. MALACHI	REV. 22
16. AMOS 7, 8, 9	REV. 7		

Appendix D
Recommended Reading List

⸲⸲⸲⸲⸲⸲⸲⸲⸲⸲⸲⸲⸲⸲⸲⸲⸲⸲⸲⸲⸲⸲ ⸜⸝ ⸲⸲⸲⸲⸲⸲⸲⸲⸲⸲⸲⸲⸲⸲⸲⸲⸲⸲⸲⸲⸲⸲

Titles, Authors, and Publishers

Section 1

TITLE	AUTHOR	PUBLISHER
1. *Knowing God*	J. I. Packer	InterVarsity Press
2. *Foundations of the Christian Faith*	James Montgomery Boice	InterVarsity Press
3. *Names of God*	Nathan Stone	Moody Press
4. *The Glory of Christ*	Peter Lewis	Moody Press
5. *The Mystery of the Holy Spirit*	R. C. Sproul	Tyndale House
6. *The Divine Inspiration of the Bible*	Arthur W. Pink	Baker Book House
7. *Essential Truths of the Christian Faith*	R. C. Sproul	Tyndale House

Section 2

TITLE	AUTHOR	PUBLISHER
8. *The Serpent of Paradise*	Erwin W. Lutzer	Moody Press
9. *The Vanishing Conscience*	John F. MacArthur, Jr.	Word
10. *The Glory of Christ*	R. C. Sproul	Tyndale House
11. *The Cross of Christ*	John R. W. Stott	InterVarsity Press
12. *He Still Moves Stones*	Max Lucado	Word
13. *Faith Works*	John F. MacArthur, Jr.	Word
14. *A New Birth*	J. C. Ryle	Baker Book House

Section 3

TITLE	AUTHOR	PUBLISHER
15. *One Minute After You Die*	Erwin Lutzer	Moody Press
16. *How to Worship Jesus Christ*	Joseph Carroll	Moody Press
17. *Living by the Book*	Howard G. Hendricks & William D. Hendricks	Moody Press
18. *Daily with the King*	W. Glyn Evans	Moody Press
19. *Abba Father*	R. Kent Hughes	Crossway Books
20. *God Up Close*	Doug McIntosh	Moody Press

Section 4

TITLE	AUTHOR	PUBLISHER
21. *Money, Possessions and Eternity*	Randy Alcorn	Tyndale House
22. *The Five Love Languages*	Gary Chapman	Moody Press
23. *Lasting Love*	Alistair Begg	Moody Press
24. *Home with a Heart*	James Dobson	Tyndale House
25. *The Pursuit of God*	A. W. Tozer	Christian Publications
26. *Explaining Your Faith*	Alister McGrath	Baker Book House

Section 5

TITLE	AUTHOR	PUBLISHER
27. *Spiritual Disciplines for the Christian Life*	Donald S. Whitney	NavPress
28. *Choices for a Lifetime*	Stuart Briscoe	Tyndale House
29. *Life's Little Instruction Book*	H. Jackson Brown, Jr.	Rutledge Hill Press
30. *Disciplines of a Godly Man*	R. Kent Hughes	Crossway Books

31.	*Sgt. York: His Life, Legend & Legacy*	John Perry	Broadman & Holman
32.	*Finding the Career That Fits You*	Lee Ellis & Larry Burkett	Moody Press
33.	*A Case for Calling*	Dr. Thomas Addington & Dr. Stephen Graves	Cornerstone Alliance

Section 6

	TITLE	AUTHOR	PUBLISHER
34.	*Living the Life You Were Meant to Live*	Tom Paterson	Thomas Nelson
35.	*Made for His Pleasure*	Alistair Begg	Moody Press
36.	*Nine Empowering Secrets of Successful Living*	Denis Waitley	Thomas Nelson
37.	*Timing Is Everything*	Denis Waitley	Thomas Nelson
38.	*Your Work Matters to God*	Doug Sherman & William Hendricks	NavPress
39.	*Ordering Your Private World*	Gordon MacDonald	Thomas Nelson
40.	*The Time Trap*	Alec Mackenzie	Amacom

Section 7

	TITLE	AUTHOR	PUBLISHER
41.	*The Books You Read*	Charles E. Jones (Editor)	Executive Books
42.	*How to Keep a Spiritual Journal*	Ronald Klug	Thomas Nelson
43.	*Organize Yourself!*	Ronni Eisenberg	Macmillan
44.	*How to Manage Your Money*	Larry Burkett	Moody Press
45.	*It's Better to Believe*	Kenneth H. Cooper, M.D.	Thomas Nelson
46.	*How to Study*	Ron Fry	Career Press

Section 8

	TITLE	AUTHOR	PUBLISHER
47.	Balancing the Christian Life	Charles C. Ryrie	Moody Press
48.	The ABC's of Wisdom	Ray Pritchard	Moody Press
49.	Celebration of Discipline	Richard J. Foster	Harper San Francisco
50.	The Power of Commitment	Jerry White	NavPress
51.	Lincoln	David Herbert Donald	Simon & Schuster
52.	Far from Home	Joseph M. Stowell	Moody Press

Appendix E
Scripture Verses by Topic

····················· ⚭ ·····················

Section 1

Topic	Book of the Bible	Translation
1. God	Genesis 1:1	NASB, NIV, NKJV, NLT
2. The Trinity	Genesis 1:26	NKJV
3. Names & Attributes of God	Exodus 3:14	NKJV
4. The Lord Jesus Christ	Colossians 1:15–16	NKJV
5. The Holy Spirit	Galatians 5:16	NLT
6. The Bible	Isaiah 40:8	NASB
7. Doctrine	2 Timothy 3:16	NKJV

Section 2

Topic	Book of the Bible	Translation
8. The Fall	Romans 3:10–11	NKJV
9. Sin	Romans 3:23	NKJV
10. The Incarnation	John 1:14	NKJV
11. The Crucifixion	John 3:16	NKJV
12. The Resurrection	John 11:25	NKJV
13. The Gospel	Romans 1:16	NKJV
14. The New Birth	John 3:3	NKJV

Section 3

Topic	Book of the Bible	Translation
15. Eternity	Colossians 3:1–3	NLT
16. Worship	1 Chronicles 16:29	NLT

· · · · ·

17. Bible Study	2 Timothy 2:15	NASB
18. Time Out with God	Psalm 46:10	NKJV
19. Talking with God	James 5:16	NLT
20. Thinking About God	Joshua 1:8	NKJV

Section 4

TOPIC	BOOK OF THE BIBLE	TRANSLATION
21. Stewardship	Matthew 6:19–21	NLT
22. Love	1 Corinthians 13:4–5	NLT
23. Marriage	Genesis 2:24	NIV
24. Family	Deuteronomy 11:18–21	NLT
25. Relationships	Mark 12:29–31	NLT
26. Sharing Your Faith	1 Peter 3:15	NIV

Section 5

TOPIC	BOOK OF THE BIBLE	TRANSLATION
27. Getting Started	Ecclesiastes 9:10	NIV
28. Developing Good Habits	Daniel 6:10	NLT
29. The Little Things	Matthew 25:21	NIV
30. Discipline	1 Timothy 4:7	NIV
31. Focus	Proverbs 4:25–26	NLT
32. Gifts and Abilities	1 Peter 4:10	NLT
33. A Calling	Romans 12:6	NLT

Section 6

TOPIC	BOOK OF THE BIBLE	TRANSLATION
34. A Mission Statement	Proverbs 4:23	NLT
35. Life Goals	2 Corinthians 5:9	NLT
36. Goal Setting	Psalm 25:4	NLT
37. Planning	Proverbs 14:8	NIV
38. Work	Genesis 2:15	NASB

39. Leisure	Genesis 2:2–3	NLT
40. Time Management	Ephesians 5:15–16	NIV

Section 7

TOPIC	BOOK OF THE BIBLE	TRANSLATION
41. Reading	2 Timothy 4:13	NLT
42. Journaling	2 Corinthians 10:4–5	NKJV
43. Organizing	Proverbs 21:5	NLT
44. Budgeting	Luke 12:42–44	NLT
45. Diet and Exercise	1 Timothy 4:8	NLT
46. Studying	Acts 17:11	NLT

Section 8

TOPIC	BOOK OF THE BIBLE	TRANSLATION
47. Balance	Proverbs 3:6	NASB
48. Moderation	Ecclesiastes 5:12	NLT
49. Simplicity	Matthew 6:33	NKJV
50. Commitment	Deuteronomy 6:5	NIV
51. Perseverance	1 Corinthians 15:58	RSV
52. Contentment	Hebrews 13:5	NKJV

Notes

Notes

Notes

Notes

Moody Press, a ministry of Moody Bible Institute,
is designed for education, evangelization, and edification.
If we may assist you in knowing more about Christ
and the Christian life, please write us without obligation:
Moody Press, c/o MLM, Chicago, Illinois 60610.